KW-480-886

Contents

Preface

This book is an introduction to Prolog intended for those who have not yet bought Prolog (either as a piece of software or as a new way of looking at computer programming) but want to find out how it works and also for those wondering whether they should use Prolog in an application. It assumes no knowledge of Prolog and very little knowledge of other computer languages.

We have deliberately tried to produce a short text. The idea is to give you a good feel for the language and leave it to you to assess the potential of Prolog for meeting your requirements. The book is divided into two parts. Part One explains the basic concepts incorporated into almost all implementations of Prolog. Part Two shows examples and areas in which Prolog shows itself in the best light (with the exception of the chapter on operators which is used to enable the meta-level expert system to be developed). We wish you a short but hopefully enjoyable read.

Acknowledgements

This project is one of the results of a period of industrial secondment which I spent at Expert Systems International Ltd. (ESI). As with software products we have produced, this book incorporates the work of the whole company. In particular, I am grateful to Tony Dodd, Carlton McDonald and Jocelyn Paine who helped me a great deal while I was with ESI.

M.Y.

I am extremely grateful to Masoud Yazdani who encouraged me to contribute to this book, despite the fact that I was inundated with many other things. The experience of co-authoring has enabled me to commit to paper ideas that I may never have made time to share. I would also like to thank the research teams at Oxford Polytechnic and the Open University for being both helpful and inspiring. Finally, I would like to thank my mother, whose example of diligence and perseverance I have tried to emulate.

C. M.

Introduction

Prolog is both a new programming language and a new way of looking at programming. Most other programming languages, such as BASIC and Pascal present the computer with the solution to a problem in the form of a series of instructions to the machine to be executed strictly in the order in which they are specified.

PROgramming in LOGic (PROLOG) should be declarative, a program should simply be the statement of the problem. The way the problem is solved and the sequences of instructions that the computer must go through to solve it, are decided by the system.

We use the word 'should' because there is no way one could stop people misusing Prolog and using it as if it was Pascal, or any other programming language that they may be familiar with. If they do this, they lose the benefits which declarative programming offers.

On the face of it, there is no reason why one would want to use a programming language other than Prolog! It is easier to say what we want done and leave it to the computer to do it for us. Computers would then be humanity's corporate slaves !

The problem with Prolog, and any other mechanical slave, is that unless one is absolutely clear as to what one wants, one is going to get piles of rubbish. In many cases people find it easier to show someone how a job is to be done and leave the slave to imitate them. This is why most professional programmers (Kay, 1984) suffer a culture shock when they first use Prolog. They have been brain washed into expecting to show the computer what to do in a great deal of detail. With Prolog they see magic things happening during the first half hour and then spend the rest of their time undoing the power of Prolog in order to make it similar to one of the programming languages they know and love. On the other hand total novices spend a great deal longer learning everything about Prolog and piggy backing on its power for a long time to come.

Prolog was born within the realm of Artificial Intelligence (AI). AI is concerned with the design and the study of the properties of intelligent systems. Human behaviour (understanding language, perception, learning, reasoning and so on) is something with which we associate intelligence. AI involves manipulating symbolic representations instead of number crunching. LISt Processing (LISP) is the oldest programming language for AI. LISP is similar in its philosophy to Pascal and other procedural languages, in as much as a program is built out of a series of instructions on how to perform a task.

Prolog originally became popular with AI researchers, as they seemed to know more about what intelligent behaviour is than how it is achieved. Prolog has therefore become a serious competitor to LISP. However, it soon became clear that there are many other problem areas in which we know more about the what than the how.

The philosophy behind Prolog (i.e. both the logical and declarative aspects) is for academics the real power. At present, the commercial world looks at speed of performance as a major criterion. The Prolog concept will come into its own with the use of parallel architectures, as Prolog solves problems by searching a knowledge base (or more correctly a database) the search will be greatly improved if several processors are made to search different parts of the database.

Prolog is an ideal prototyping language because of the speed with which a system can be developed (partly because of the interpretive nature of the language, other factors include the declarative nature, the compactness and inherent modularity of Prolog programs). Once the developer has satisfied the customer that the system is feasible, a conventional procedural language is often used. Even though Prolog compilers do exist their use is still not widespread outside of academia.

A Prolog program consists of a collection of two types of entity:

a) facts

and

b) rules.

This collection is known as the *database*. When the database has been set up, it is then possible to ask if certain things are true, given the facts and rules of the database.

Facts are statements that are known unconditionally to be true, such as:

Socrates is a man.

Rules are conditional facts. Such as:

If someone is a man then he is mortal.

Assume that we have given Prolog this information and we are happy with its correctness. We can then ask Prolog the question:

Is Socrates mortal ?

Prolog will answer

yes.

This **yes** is an indication that in the context of the given facts the query is true. Suppose we now ask Prolog another question:

Is Tony mortal?

Prolog will answer

no.

Prolog is only able to answer yes or no. In this case, it lacks certain information on Tony and so is unable to prove that Tony is mortal. As far as Prolog is concerned, this is untrue.

In Prolog, <u>no</u> should be interpreted as meaning; 'Given the information I have, I am unable to prove this to be true'.

Given, this simple way of writing a program and a set of basic primitive facilities, which the user could incorporate into his program, Prolog can be used for a diversity of applications.

Obviously, the application needs to lend itself to Prolog's strengths. If we wish to do a great deal of calculation in order to get an answer (say in calculating income from stock market shares) then we would use a more 'traditional' language. If however, we wish to deal with less tangible, problem solving issues (such as forecasting share price fluctuations) then we might use Prolog.

Part One:

Prolog Programming

CHAPTER 1

A Simple Model for Prolog Execution

This chapter seeks to introduce the way in which Prolog programs are executed. The philosophy behind the graphical approach is that the esoteric parts of Prolog may be easier to understand if one is able to visualise what is happening. It also means that a graphical debugger could be developed in order to facilitate the development of Prolog programs. There already exists a graphical debugger produced at the Open University by Mike Brayshaw and Marc Eisenstadt, their product is called the Transparent Prolog Machine (TPM). They use a different representation to the one used here, but they have found that a graphical representation enables Prolog systems to be understood and developed a lot easier than conventional textual approaches.

Before you try the examples and exercises you will need to know how to get information into the database. The database will be all the things that the system knows. The easiest way to tell the system something is by typing:

?- **consult(user).**

Most systems allow you to shorten this by typing:

?- **[user].**

Any information which you now type in will go straight into the database. The termination of the entering of information (consultation) into the database is machine dependent, but is often the end of file key sequence for the machine (control-D for Unix systems, control-Z for IBM etc.). Unfortunately the information in the database will be lost when you exit Prolog unless you save it to a file. This will be covered later. The other alternative at this stage is to type the information into a file and consult the file rather than the user. For example suppose we had a file called 'cars' then

   ?- [cars].

would load the information in the file 'cars' into the database. The system uses the information to create a problem representation. The system solves all problems by traversing this representation of the Prolog database of facts and rules in order to determine the validity of any queries you make. All Prolog programs are expressed as facts and rules. With the exception of input (reading) and output (writing) the system does nothing except answer queries.

Facts and questions

The Prolog interpreter answers questions, but you must provide it with enough information to answer the question. For example you can ask the system if it knows about some fact. For example, suppose you told the system three facts (representing three animals cat, rat and bat). The Prolog representation is simply:

   cat.
   rat.
   bat.

These three facts are represented as three boxes in Figure 1.1. If we want to ask the system if it knows about a rat we type:

?- **rat.**

The system then looks among the boxes to see if rat is among them. If it finds it, it responds 'yes' otherwise it responds 'no'. In this case searching for **rat** it responds:

yes.

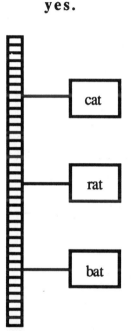

Fig. 1.1 Representation of three simple facts

The system does not know that the facts are animals and therefore cannot answer questions about the size or number of legs that the animals have. All it knows is that rat, cat and bat exist in its memory.

Rules

Sometimes it may not be possible to give the system everything in terms of facts. The system can look for other facts in order to determine whether or not a query is true. You can specify rules for the system to follow, for example if looking for the box (the fact) a, and the box is not found, then if you can find boxes b, c, and d then fact a is true. To inform the system of this rule we write in Prolog:

a :- b, c, d.

and the facts:

a .
b .
c .
d .

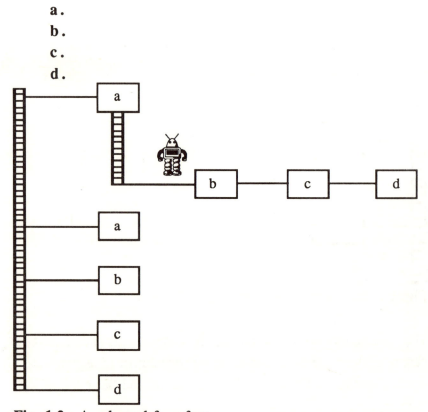

Fig. 1.2   A rule and four facts

In the rule 'a' is termed the **head goal** and the goals b, c, and d are termed the **tail goals**. This single rule and the list of facts are represented by the system diagrammatically in Figure 1.2.

The system likes climbing down stairs whenever it can, sometimes doing more work than is necessary. It needs a little tempering, so in order to stop it going off on a wild goose chase, care should be taken to give it facts before rules, as in Figure 1.3 instead of the ordering in Figure 1.4.

a .

a :- b, c, d.

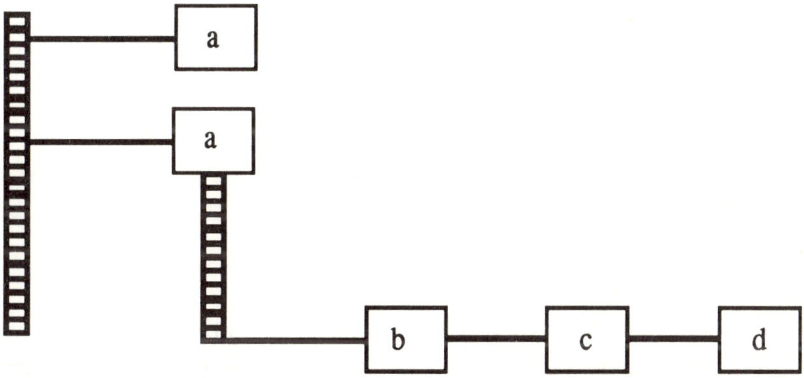

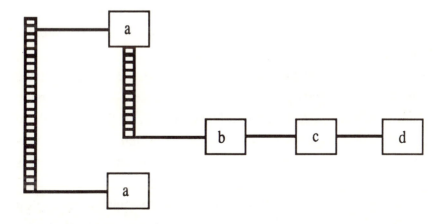

Fig. 1.3 Fact before rule.

Fig. 1.4 Rule before fact

```
a :- b, c, d.
a.
```

Flow of execution

Suppose we gave the system the following database (database 1):

```
a :- b, c, d.
b.
c :- e, f.
c :- g.
d.
e.
f.
g.
```

The system is able to represent this information in one of two ways, there is the static view of Figure 1.5 or the dynamic view of Figure 1.6. The static view of the Prolog database represents the facts and rules in a way that does not show how they interact with each other during the execution. The second representation is the dynamic view (Figure 1.6) used by the system to enable it to solve problems in a straightforward way.

The system has rules for traversing the problem space which will be made explicit later in this chapter. While traversing the problem space the system leaves a trail, so that it is able to find its way back to the top. When the system finds what it is looking for it is happy, if it is unable to find something then it is sad (see Figure 1.7).

As we are concerned with the execution of Prolog programs we will only consider the dynamic view of Prolog programs as represented by the system. All subsequent diagrammatic representations of Prolog code is the dynamic view of the Prolog database during execution with the inter-relationships of the facts and rules.

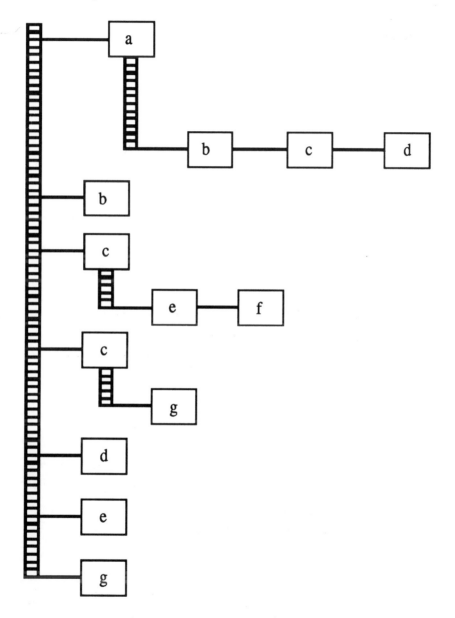

Fig. 1.5 Static view of a Prolog database as represented by Prolog

Failure

If the system in trying to find any of the boxes fails then it returns to the top level and says **no**. This means that it failed to satisfy all of the necessary intermediate goals in proving the initial query.

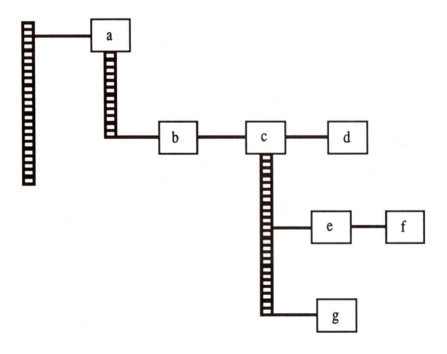

Fig. 1.6 The dynamic view of a database as represented by the system

Backtracking

If we have database 1 again except that fact f is missing, i.e. Figure 1.7

    a :- b, c, d.
    b.
    c :- e, f.

```
c :- g.
d.
e.
g.
```

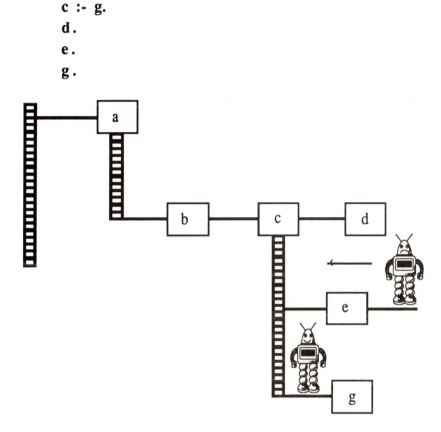

Fig. 1.7 Database 1 with fact f missing

The system in trying to satisfy c, tries to find e and f. It finds e but then does not find f. It returns sadly until it realises that it has another way of trying to satisfy c, it climbs down the ladder and finds g, thereby satisfying c. This process of going over old ground is termed *backtracking*.

As another example suppose we have the same database 1 as before except that fact d is missing, i.e. Figure 1.8.

The Prolog representation is:

```
a :- b, c, d.
b.
c :- e, f.
c :- g.
d.
e.
g.
```

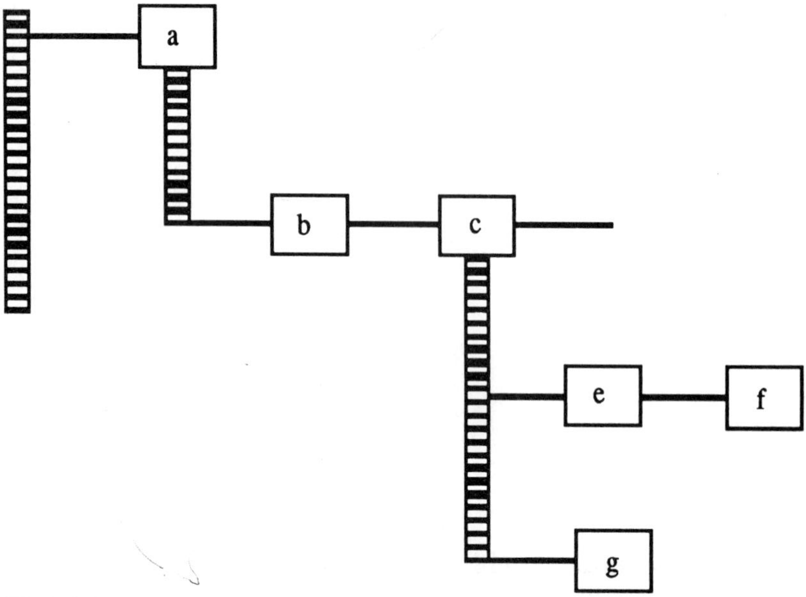

Fig. 1.8 Database 1 with fact d missing

The system, in trying to prove the top level goal **a**, finds b, e and f which satisfy c, but fails to find d. At this point it **backtracks** to try and find another way of satisfying any of the previous goals. This has no effect upon the final outcome but as will be seen later when it deals with variables backtracking may lead to a solution with another variable. When any of the tail goals in the toplevel call fail to be satisfied then the toplevel call will always fail, regardless of whether backtracking takes place or not; or whether variables are being used or not.

The cut

You can stop the system from backtracking by using a cut (an exclamation mark) to fail the parent goal, for example:

w :- x, !, y, z.
w :- p, q.

The system representation is shown below in Figure 1.9. with a rope ladder that can only be used when going from left to right (backtracking).

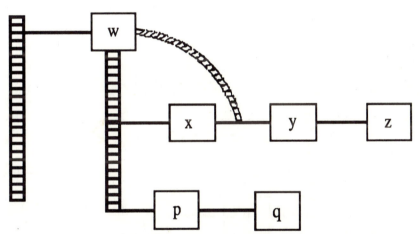

Fig. 1.9 The diagrammatic representation of the cut

The cut not only prevents the system from trying to resatisfy the parent goal (w in the previous example), but it also prevents him trying to resatisfy x. For instance suppose in addition to the two w clauses in the previous example we have two ways of satisfying x, i.e we now have:

w :- x, !, y, z.
w :- p, q.
x :- a.

x :- b.

a.

b.

The cut also prevents the resatisfaction of x. The system's representation is shown below in Figure 1.10.

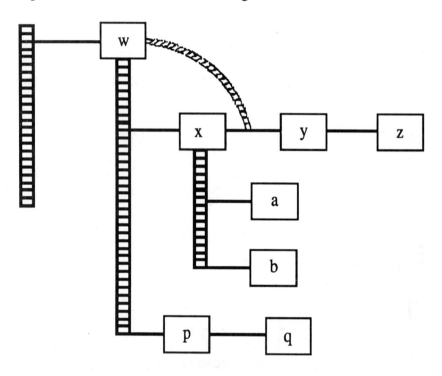

Fig. 1.10 Preventing backtracking

Example

a :- b, c, d.

b.

c :- e, !, f.

c :- g.

d.

e.

f.

g.

The diagrammatic representation is shown below in Figure 1.11. If the system fails to find f this time, then the search for goal a will fail.

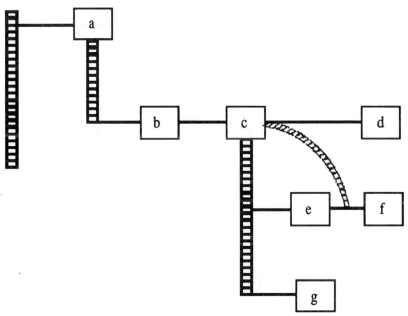

Fig. 1.11 Effects of the cut on execution

There are four rules that the system has for passing ladders:

    1. If walking to the right go down the ladder

    2. If walking right never go up the ladder

    3. If **sadly** walking left go down in preference to going up the ladder

    4. If contentedly walking left always go up the ladder

Why stop the system backtracking ?

Consider the following:

```
even_number :-
        number,                 /* Do not backtrack */
        !,                      /* past the cut goal */
        divisible_by_2.         /* if divisible by 2 */
even_number :- 2.
even_number :- 4.
        .

        .

even_number :- 1234567890.
```

The system's representation is shown below in Figure 1.12.

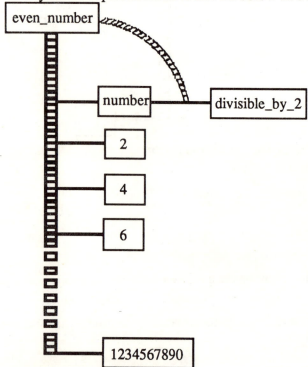

Fig. 1.12 Example of the cut at work

Variables

So far we have only looked at simple facts without relationships. The goals have been Prolog *atoms*. Prolog atoms are any combination of letters, digits and underscore characters beginning with a lowercase letter. We have the ability to reason about relations as well. Suppose we had the database:

animal(bat).	/* a bat is an animal */
animal(rat).	/* a rat is an animal */
animal(cat).	/* a cat is an animal */

The system ignores anything between '/*' and '*/' which is the way that comments are made and represents the above database in the following way in Figure 1.13

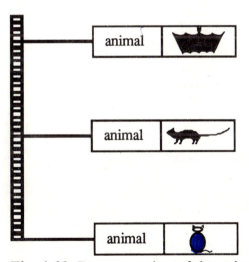

Fig. 1.13 Representation of the animal database

We could then ask the system the following questions:

?- **animal(cat).**   /* is a cat an animal ? */

To which the system responds

yes.

Prolog is able to provide multiple solutions if they exist. Using the animal database of Figure 1.13 the query below generates three solutions.

For this query, and subsequent examples requiring multiple solutions to a query in some implementations of Prolog you will not be prompted with the **'more y/n'** prompt but you can achieve the same effect (i.e. producing several solutions) by typing a semicolon instead of the 'y'.

?- **animal(X).**   /* is X an animal ? */

In response to this question the system says:

X = bat
more y/n ?   if we respond 'y'

the system says:

X = rat
more y/n ?   if we respond 'y' again

the system says:

X = cat
more y/n ?   this time when we respond 'y'

the system says:

no.

because there are no more animals that can be found.

Take as a final example the following database, which you should create using an editor.

```
tame(X) :-                          /* X is tame if */
    animal(X),                 /* X is an animal and */
    legs(X,4),                    /* X has 4 legs */
    on(X,mat).                   /* X is on the mat */


animal(rat).                    /* rat is an animal */
animal(bat).                    /* bat is an animal */
animal(cat).                    /* cat is an animal */


legs(bat,  2).                 /* a bat has 2 legs */
legs(cat,  4).                 /* a cat has 4 legs */
legs(rat,  4).                 /* a rat has 4 legs */


on(X, Y) :-                         /* X is on Y if */
    at(X,  Y).                       /* X is at Y */


at(rat,  hole).              /* rat is at the hole */
at(bat,  cave).              /* bat is at the cave */
at(cat,  mat).               /* cat is at the mat */
```

Then tell the system to consult the file for information, i.e.

```
?- [filename].
```

The system's representation of this information is illustrated in Figure 1.14.

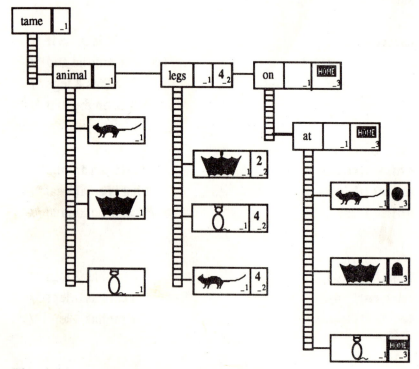

Fig. 1.14 A more complicated database

The system represents variables internally using an underscore character followed by an integer. The numbers are allocated arbitrarily and do not mean anything, but whenever you trace your program on most systems your variables will appear in the form

_246, _10109... etc.

In tracing the execution you could regard the variable numbers as pages in a photo album. So that as well as trying to find boxes, the system also tries to find photos that match those on the pages of its photo album. In the above example the system has three pages of photographs (1 photo per page) to fill and match consistently.

Consider the query

   ?- tame(Pet).   /* can you find a tame pet ? */

The execution can be described in terms of what the system does at each stage during the execution. The first page of the album has a picture of a *rat* inserted when it finds the **animal** box. The system uses this to record the value of a variable and the process of putting a picture into its album is called *instantiation*. The system remembers where it picked up the pictures so that when it backtracks it knows where to replace pictures or give up looking. When it goes on to the **legs** box it has a blank page to match with. The number of the page indicates to the system where to look in order to find a copy of the picture. The first page of the album has a picture of a *rat* put into the first page when the system finds the first **animal** box (instantiation). When the system goes on to the **legs** box it finds a blank page where the system has its picture of a *rat*. A copy of the *rat* is put in the blank page. It then tries to find a *rat* with *4* **legs**, as the second page of the **legs** album already has a picture of *4* there. After encountering a *rat* and a *cat* eventually a *rat* is found and it also has *4* legs. The system returns to the **legs** box happy because it has found everything that it has been looking for so far.

  The system moves along to the **on** box, the first page is again blank where it has a picture of a *rat*. It is now searching for a *rat* on a *mat*. Descending the ladder reveals an **at** box with a blank page where it has a picture of a *rat*, it leaves a copy of the *rat* in the _1 slot of the **at** box. It now has to find a *rat* at a *mat* in order to prove **on** *rat mat* which is the last clause in finding a **tame animal**.

The system first finds a *rat* which matches the first page of its album, next it has to examine the third page of the album in order to complete its search. The third page of the **at** box does not match the system's. It has failed to find the *rat* on a *mat* here because both pictures did not match. It tries the next boxes but the first page does not even match so it does not bother to check the third pages in the *bat* and *cat* albums.

The system now backtracks trying to find an alternative **tame animal**, but it does as little reworking as possible. Firstly, it removes the *rat* pictures from the **at** and **on** boxes, eventually it returns to the **legs** box to see if it can find anymore *rats* with *4* legs. Of course, it fails to find any more and so it also removes the *rat* picture from the first page of the album in the **legs** box. If it did find another *rat* with *4* legs it would have continued, to try and find a *rat* on a *mat*. It does not have the ability to remember what it has tried. The system has been designed to make sure that all possibilities are sought. So that if a solution exists then it will find it. Efficiency is not in its vocabulary. This approach enables the system to find as many solutions as exist if required.

The system now returns to the **animal** box and remembers that it was here that the *rat* came from, but before it arrived at the **animal** box its album was empty. It removes the copy of the *rat* from the **animal** box, and tries to find another **animal** as it descends the ladder from the *rat*. This time it finds a *bat*, puts a picture of the *bat* in the first page of its album and then returns to the **animal** box placing a copy of the *bat* picture in the album there.

When it arrives at the **legs** box this time, the first page of its album has a picture of a *bat*, which it copies and puts in the first page of the **legs** album. It seeks an album with a *bat* on the first page and a picture of *2* **legs** on the second page. It finds the *bat* on the first page of the first album it tries under the **legs** box, but the second page does not match. It then tries to find another *bat* (just in case there is one with *4 legs*) but only finds a *cat* and a *rat*. The system backtracks yet again, removing the picture of the *bat* from the **legs** and **animal** boxes. The system does not get tired or fed up but descends the ladder again and continues searching at the point immediately after the *bat*. It does not know what comes next and has to descend the ladder before it finds the *cat*.

A picture of the *cat* is put in the **animal** box, as well as in the first page of its photo album. For the third time (plus two backtrackings) the system returns to the **legs** box. it puts a copy of the cat picture in the first page of the **legs** album, proceeding to search for a *cat* with *4 legs*. This time it is successful, and progresses to the **on** box again placing a picture of the *cat* in the first page of the album. It finds that there is a picture of a *mat* in the third page and puts a copy into the third page of its own album, before starting to search for a *cat* **on** a *mat*. The search for a *cat* **on** a *mat* leads to a search of a *cat* **at** a *mat*. The system installs a copy of the *cat* in the first page of the **at** box. It checks the first page of the next two albums and fails to find a picture of a *cat*. The third attempt is successful. The system proceeds to try and match the third pages as well, which it does successfully. It then returns to the top level having found a **tame animal**. It then reports success by saying:

Pet = cat

The important points to note here are:

➤ The Prolog system has the ability to remember where it got its pictures from. Prolog execution automatically resets variables at the right places.

➤ The system does not know how many solutions exist until

it actually tries to descend the ladders. Prolog always backtracks even if there are no more solutions.

➤ The search strategy is exhaustive, finding a solution if one exists.

➤ The search of the database is completely blind, it faithfully follows a depth first search strategy. On large problems the system requires a lot of space to make a note of the different variables and where their values originated.

➤ The execution can be made more efficient by the use of careful ordering of information and cut statements.

Summary

*   The order in which facts appear in the Prolog database determines the order in which solution to the problems are sought, and the order of instantiation of variables.

*   Whenever the system goes along a path and fails to find a solution it does not give up, it backtracks to a ladder and sees if it is able to go down and find a potential solution.

*   If in the process of bactracking the system encounters a cut, then it abandons the parent goal (the goal that initiated the search at the level at which the system failed to find a solution) not the whole execution.

Exercise

1.   How may the ordering of the clauses in the **tame** example be reordered to make the execution more efficient ?

CHAPTER 2

Terms

Any item of data, be it a clause in the database or a data structure is referred to as a **term**. The simplest form of Prolog term is the **atom**. Atoms may be added to the database and questions can be asked about them. The syntax of atoms is any sequence of lower case letters, underscore characters and numbers beginning with a lower case letter. For example all of the following three terms are atoms:

cat
rat
bat

More complex terms may be constructed and the rules of construction are found in the following section on structures. The difference between a term and a clause is that a clause is a term terminated by a period. Queries are clauses which are matched against the database, which is itself a collection of clauses.

Structures

The syntax of a Prolog structure is an atom, followed by any number of arguments in parentheses. Each of the arguments is itself a Prolog term. There is a convention which can be followed to make Prolog structures and programs more readable. Let us first have a look at some examples of structures. The general form is:

structure(Arg1, Arg2, ... , Argn).

Some specific examples are

> **big(mac).**
> **fat(humpty_dumpty).**

The way that these relations are interpreted is for unary relations of the form

> **structure(Arg).**

Arg is structure. Using the examples above the interpretation is

> mac is big   and   humpty_dumpty is fat.

Binary relations of the form:

> **structure(Arg1, Arg2).**

are interpreted

> Arg1 structure Arg2

for example,

> /* the Queen lives at Buckingham Palace */
> **lives(queen, buckingham_palace).**
>
> /* Miss Piggy likes Kermit */
> **likes(miss_piggy, kermit).**
>
> **on(cat, mat).**   /* the cat is on the mat */

This does not exclude relations of the form

partners(bill, ben).   /* bill & ben are partners */

but even this can be written as a relation of the form Arg1 structure Arg2, i.e.

partner(bill, ben).   /* bill is the partner of ben */
                                 /* OR bill's partner is ben */

You can see from these simple examples that there is a variety of ways that a relation can be read.   As Prolog tends to be a collection of many relations in a database, there is ample opportunity for errors unless some convention is adhered to consistently. If everyone tried to write their Prolog code in this manner, using meaningful variable names, then we would be closer to achieving our goal of declarative programming.

The ability to construct data structures is a powerful problem solving tool. Prolog programs support all the features of a good software engineering tool, namely: modularity, readability, data structures, abstraction and information hiding. There are, however, no data types. The ability to perceive Prolog programs in term of what they do as opposed to how they do them means that predicates (subprograms) can be read and understood declaratively. This separation lends itself to top-down design, but as Prolog is easy to read, the development of a program by first writing the top-level calls, and then writing the lower level routines means that we can use Prolog as our design language as well. These features contribute to the use of Prolog as a very quick and powerful prototyping tool.

Declarative programming

Prolog allows the programmer to express facts and rules in a logical way, such that the declaration of relationships may be used to determine the truth of a query. For example:

> Mum is the mother of Child if
>> Mum is female and
>> Dad is the father of Child and
>> Dad married Mum

The order of the clauses can be changed while preserving the validity of the truth. This rule can be directly translated into Prolog:

```
mother(Mum, Child) :- /* Mum is mother of Child if */
    female(Mum),              /* Mum is female & */
    father(Dad, Child),   /* Dad is father of Child & */
    married(Dad, Mum).   /* Dad is married to Mum */
```

The ':-' at the end of the first line is read as 'if'. It separates the clause:head of the clause from the tail goals. The ',' at the end of each of the tail goals is read as 'and'; its role is to separate each of the tail goals. The full stop is the terminator of the clause.

Royal Database

```
male(edward).                 male(philip).
male(george5).                male(george6).
male(charles).                male(andrew).
male(mark).                   male(anthony).
male(william).                male(harry).


female(liz1).                 female(liz2).
female(anne).                 female(sarah).
female(margaret).             female(mary).
female(lady_di).
```

```
father(philip, charles).        /* Philip is the father of Charles */
father(philip, andrew).         /* Philip is the father of Andrew */
father(philip, anne).           /* Philip is the father of Anne */
father(philip, edward).         /* Philip is the father of Edward */
father(george6, margaret).  /* George 6th is father of Margaret */
father(george6, liz2).      /* George 6th, father of Elizabeth 1st */
father(george5, george6).   /* George 5th father of George 6th */
father(anthony, sarah).         /* Anthony is the father of Sarah */
father(charles, william).     /* Charles is the father of William */
father(charles, harry).        /* Charles is the father of Harry */


married(philip, liz2).            /* Philip married Elizabeth 2nd */
married(george6, liz1).     /* George 6th married Elizabeth 1st */
married(mark, anne).                    /* Mark married Anne */
married(anthony, margaret).      /* Anthony married Margaret */
married(george5, mary).           /* George 5th married Mary */
married(charles, lady_di).            /* Charles married Di */
```

Fig. 2.1. Royal family database

Programming is an art which is best learnt by doing. Only by
trying the examples out on a computer will the power and
simplicity of Prolog be appreciated. The royal family database of
Figure 2.1 has been provided for you to determine what the
relationships between members of the royal family are. Type in
the database, and type in the mother predicate above and see if
you can find all the mothers using the query:

    ?- **mother(Mummy, _).**

You could find all of Elizabeth II children by typing in the query:

    ?- **mother(liz2, Heir).**

Let us have a look at another example. We want to write the brother relationship, which we will first express in English:

> Bro is the brother of Sib if
>> Bro is male and
>> Dad is the father of Bro and
>> Dad is the father of Sib and
>> Mum is the mother of Bro and
>> Mum is the mother of Sib

The only problem here is that Bro and Sib denote variables (representing brother and sibling respectively) and there is no reason why they may not be instantiated to the same thing, thereby representing the same person. To complete the predicate we need to say:

> Bro is not equal to Sib

Translating into Prolog we get:

```
brother(Bro, Sib) :-    /* Bro is the brother of Sib if */
    male(Bro),                      /* Bro is male and */
    father(Dad, Bro),  /* Dad is the father of Bro and */
    father(Dad, Sib),   /* Dad is the father of Sib and */
    mother(Mum, Bro),  /* Mum is mother of Bro & */
    mother(Mum, Sib), /* Mum is mother of Sib and */
    Bro  \= Sib.    /* Bro and Sib not the same person */
```

Notice that we have used the relationship 'mother' which we defined as a predicate. In Prolog queries may be answered by consulting facts or rules in the database. There is no priority given to one over the other, what matters is the order of the clauses (facts and rules) in the database that match the query.

Disjunctions

As a final example let us develop the predicate 'uncle'. The first step is to write the natural language representation:

> Uncle is the uncle of Person if
>> Uncle is male and
>> Uncle is the brother of Mum and
>> Mum is the mother of Person
>
> or
>
>> Uncle is male and
>> Uncle is the brother of Dad and
>> Dad is the father of Person

This can be translated into Prolog:

```
uncle(Uncle, Person) :-
    male(Uncle),
    brother(Uncle, Dad),
    father(Dad, Person).
uncle(Uncle, Person) :-
    male(Uncle),
    brother(Uncle, Mum),
    mother(Mum, Person).
```

The 'or' in the natural language description of the relationship is implicit in the disjunction of the two rules. An uncle can be proven from either of the two rules. There can be any number of choices, each should have its own rule that will be tried if the preceding ones fail.

The astute amongst you will have realised that there is a better way to write the uncle predicate. If we write a predicate parent (where a parent is a mother or a father) then the predicate becomes:

```
parent(Pa, child) :- father(Pa, Child).
parent(Ma, child) :- mother(Ma, Child).

uncle(Uncle, Person) :-
   male(Uncle),
   parent(Parent, Person),
   brother(Uncle, Parent).
```

This is better software engineering. The solution has a higher level of abstraction and is therefore easier to understand. These solutions are not always easy to detect, and again practice is the key to success. There is one more refinement that can be made. The parent predicate can be written:

```
parent(Parent, Child) :-/* Parent is parent of Child if */
    mother(Parent, Child) ;    /* mother of Child or */
    father(Parent, Child).          /* father of Child */
```

Here, the semicolon is read as 'or'. The semicolon however is not a reliable operator to use, and if we try and rewrite the uncle predicate as it first appeared we would get into problems, i.e.

```
uncle(Uncle, Person) :-
   male(Uncle),
   brother(Uncle, Dad),
   father(Dad, Person) ;          /* disjunction here */
   male(Uncle),
   brother(Uncle, Mum),
   mother(Mum, Person).
```

does not do what you expect. The reason for this is the way in which the operator ';' has been declared in relation to the comma operator (see chapter on operators). Some guidelines on the use of the semicolon:

1. Use the semicolon only when there are exclusively disjunctive subgoals.
2. If two clauses differ by a single subgoal then the clause may be rewritten with the difference disjoined within parentheses, e.g.:

```
uncle(Uncle, Person) :-
   male(Uncle),
   brother(Uncle, Sibling),
   (
      father(Sibling,Person)
      ;
      mother(Sibling,Person)
   ).
```

It is however, from the point of readability, better to have a separate predicate to deal with the disjunction. In the above example the parent predicate would handle the disjunction for us, i.e.

```
uncle(Uncle, Person) :-
   male(Uncle),
   brother(Uncle, Sibling),
   parent(Sibling, Person).
```

Summary

In this chapter we learnt

* How to write declarative routines
* How and when to use disjunctions
* Conventions for making Prolog programs more readable

Exercises

1. Express in Prolog the following natural language relationship

> Sis is the sister of Sib if
>> Sis is female and
>> Dad is the father of Sis and
>> Dad is the father of Sib and
>>> Mum is the mother of Sis and
>>> Mum is the mother of Sib

2.   Write the natural language statement of the following relationships and then translate them into Prolog. You would be advised to use relations already defined, e.g. brother and sister.

> a) sibling(Sib, Person).
> b) cousin(Cuzz, Person).
> c) niece(Niece, Person).
> d) grandfather(Grand_pa, Child).
> e) grandmother(Grand_ma, Child).
> f) aunt(Aunty, Person).

You will find that by writing the English statement of the relationship the solution in Prolog is much more straightforward. If the system that you are building is going to take more than two or three hours to build it is worthwhile writing a natural language statement for all predicates, this discipline will save time in the overall development.

CHAPTER 3

Input and Output

The simplest way to output something is to **'write'** it. The predicate **write** takes one argument, and prints it out at the terminal. If the argument is uninstantiated then a unique variable will be printed out, **e.g. '_123'.** **write** succeeds only once and cannot be undone on backtracking. For example:

> ?- **write('Prolog is brilliant').**

output on the screen will be:

Prolog is brilliant

The statement:

> ?- write(L).

produces the following output depending upon what L is instantiated to.

instantiation	output
L = a	a
L = 34	34
L = peter	peter
where L is uninstantiated	_456 (or some other number)

Input

In order to input information data is **read** from the current input stream (see I/O streams later in this chapter).

read(X).

The predicate **'read',** takes a Prolog term from the computer terminals keyboard. The term must be followed by a full stop **'.'** **and** a carriage return. **X** may be instantiated or uninstantiated. If the argument is uninstantiated then **X** will be instantiated to the argument entered at the terminal. This is the way that read is normally used, but it may be used to check for a particular user response by instantiating **X**, e.g.

   ?- **read(yes)**

then the goal will succeed if the user enters **'yes.'**. **read** succeeds only once and cannot be undone on backtracking.

Outputing/writing single characters

Characters are treated as single characters corresponding to the **ascii** code for that character.

   The predicate **'put'** takes a single argument which must be a single character i.e. the ascii code for that character, then **put** writes that character to the current output stream. **put** succeeds only once and cannot be undone on backtracking.

   ?- **put(115),put(116),put(111),put(112).**

the Prolog system responds

stop
yes.

> ?- **put(c).**

no.

There is a built in predicate (see chapter 5 for built in predicates) **nl** which causes a new line (carriage return followed by a line feed) to be output.

Reading a single character

A character can be read in from the keyboard using the goals **get(X)** and **get0(X)**. If **X** is uninstantiated then the goal always succeeds. Whenever the goal is encountered the execution will not continue until a character is entered at the terminal. The difference between the two predicates is that **get(X)** will instantiate **X** to the next printing character entered i.e. any of the following

> **a . . . z**
> **0 . . . 9**
> **%, £, & @ etc.**

but **not** space, return or bell. **get0(X)** however will instantiate **X** to the ascii value of the very next key depressed, whether printing or non-printing.

I/O streams

Prolog can read from and write to files and certain devices. These can all be referred to as **streams.** The default input stream is referred to as **'user'** and takes its input from the **keyboard**. The default output stream is the **screen** and is also referred to as **'user'**. Any other input or output file or device must be opened explicitly using **'see'** for input or **'tell'** for output.

All input and output can only be taken from the current input stream and the current output streams respectively.

see

see(X) opens a file **X** for input, and causes all successive **reads** or **gets** to be taken from that file until the goal **'seen'** is encountered. Because only one input stream may be open at any instant during execution **'seen'** with no arguments simply closes the file and returns the current input stream to the default **user.**

tell

tell(X) opens a file **X** for output. All subsequent **writes, puts** and **listings** will produce output in the file **X**. The goal **'told'** completes the output and closes the file returning the current output stream to the default **'user'.**

Seeing and Telling

To find the current input stream/file the goal **seeing(X)** will instantiate **X** to the current input stream/file.

To find the current output stream/file the goal **telling(X)** will instantiate **X** to the current output stream.

Summary

I/P

read a character	**get(Char)**
read a key	**get0(Key)**
read a Prolog term terminated by a full stop	**read(String)**

O/P

write a character	**put(Char)**
write a new line (carriage return, line feed)	**nl**
write a string of characters	**write('String')**
write an atom	**write(Atom)**
o/p a number of spaces	**tab(Number)**
write a predicate	**listing(Pred)**
list all the predicates in the database	**listing**

Files

open a file for reading	**see(File)**
find the current input stream	**seeing(Input)**
close input stream	**seen**
open a file for writing	**tell(File)**
find the current output stream	**telling(Outfile)**
close output stream	**told**

Exercises

1. Write a predicate **greet** that reads a person's name and outputs that name to the keyboard e.g.

> ?- **greet.**

Who am I greeting ?

kermy.

Hello Kermy !

yes.

2. Find the ascii value of the following by reading a character and writing the ascii value to the screen.

    a) the space bar
    b) the return key
    c) the ampersand character (&)

CHAPTER 4

Lists

The basic data structure in Prolog is the list. In Prolog a list is represented as a set of elements separated by commas, e.g.:

[1, 2, 3, 4, 5]

Unlike conventional procedural languages Prolog does not make it possible to index individual elements. Instead Prolog provides a method of accessing the first element of a list. To see how and why Prolog has these seemingly annoying limitations (which is in fact its power), let us first have a look at the way in which lists are represented in Prolog.

The list above [1, 2, 3, 4, 5] is represented:

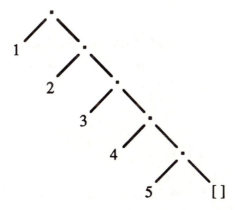

The period is an operator which takes two arguments, in actual fact this graphical representation is represented in Prolog as:

.(1, .(2, .(3, .(4, .(5, [])))))

The first argument is the atom 1, the second the structure

.(2, .(3, .(4, .(5, []))))

or in diagrammatic terms, the first argument is the left subtree

1

The second, the right subtree

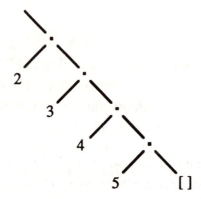

As the dot notation is awkward to use, there is a convenient way of accessing the first and last items of a list, or more accurately the **head** and **tail** of a list. If, for instance, Num is the list [1, 2, 3, 4, 5] then

Num = [Ltree | Rtree]

instantiates Ltree to 1 and Rtree to .(2, .(3, .(4, .(5, [])))) which is conveniently displayed as [2, 3, 4, 5]. The pipe operator therefore, is used to split a list into its head and tail elements, its left and right subtrees.

Notice that the structure is recursive. If we examine the tail of the list recursively then we get:

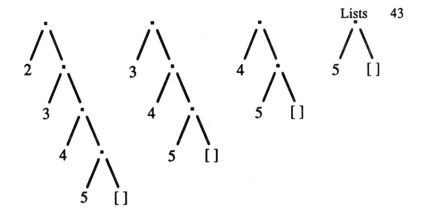

Generally speaking the head of a list is always a single item, and the tail of a list is always a list even if it is the mandatory empty list ([]). The exception to the rule of having a single item as the head of a list, is when the first item of a list is itself a list:

[[a, b], c, d]

This is a three element list, the first item of which is itself a list of two items. A pictorial representation may help here.

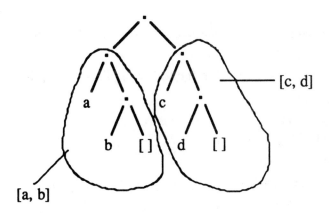

Consider as a final example the list

[[a, b], [c, d], [e, f]]
represented diagrammatically as a three element list:

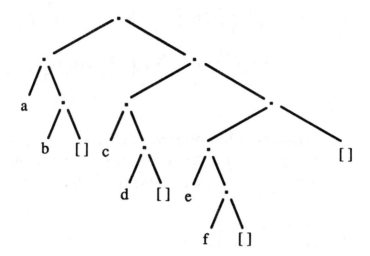

Summary

*   We looked at the syntax of lists
*   Lists are inherently recursive in structure
*   We looked at the pipe operator for splitting a list into head and tail portions of the list.

Exercise

What is the head and tail of the following lists?

```
[a, b, c]
[H, T]
[a]
[ [a, b, c] ]
[ [1, 2], [3, 4] ]
[5, [6, 7, 8] ]
[ [bat,cat,rat], [red,yellow,green], [the,quick,brown,fox] ]
```

CHAPTER 5

Built in Predicates

Built in Predicates (BIPs) may provide facilities that save a programmer from having to define their own. Two examples are **read** and **write,** the cut is also regarded as a built in predicate.

Success and failure

true always succeeds, does not do anything but may be used for readability.

fail always fails, useful for

1. producing all possible solutions

>   e.g. **muppet(X),write(X),nl,fail.**

>   prints out a list of all the muppets in the database.

2. prohibiting backtracking when used with the cut symbol.

>   e.g. **small(elephant):- !,fail.**
>   **small(X):-microscopic(X).**
>   :
>   :

If we are trying to determine whether or not something is small, then if it is an elephant **do not backtrack** because it is definitely not small.

Testing for instantiations

There are two built predicates which have been provided to test a variable (say, X) to see if it is instantiated or not:

var(X)   succeeds if X is uninstantiated

nonvar(X)   succeeds if X is instantiated

Testing for atoms

atom(X)   succeeds if X is a Prolog atom

for example:

>   ?-atom(apple).

>   yes.

>   ?- atom(789).

no.

>   ?- atom('Anything in single quotes is an atom').

>   yes.

>   ?- atom("double quotes declare strings").

>   no.

>   ?- atom(clause(Arg1,Arg2)).

no.

integer(X)	succeeds if X stands for an integer
atomic(X)	succeeds if X is either an integer or an atom
real(X)	succeeds if X is a real number
string(X)	succeeds if X is a string

Listing Prolog clauses

listing(X)

Produces a listing of all the predicates with the same name as X. X must be an atom. If for some reason you want to examine a predicate then instead of leaving Prolog and editing the file, you can list it at the terminal in order to ensure that the predicate really is as intended.

listing

Lists all the user defined clauses in the database. Useful for verifying that all predicates are in the database and all the clauses for each predicate are also present in the database. Unfortunately it is only available in some implementations.

Adding and deleting clauses from the database

To add clauses to the database, facts and rules are **asserted**

assert(X)

always succeed. The result is that X is added to the database as a
new clause. The effects cannot be undone when backtracking. If
any clause of the same name already exist in the database, then X
is asserted after all the others with the same head goal.

asserta(X)

has the same effect as assert except that X is placed before any
clauses with the same name in the database.

e.g.

1.   **assert(clause(arg, arg2)).**

2.   **asserta((rule(Conditions, Actions) :-
                satisfied(Conditions))).**

3.   **assert(sequence([1, 2, 3])).**

but not

4.   **assert(listing(fred)).**

You cannot add to system BIPs *Built in Predicate*

5.   **assert(rule(A, C) :- satisfied(C)).**

because of the operator ':-' we need to include everything in
brackets as in 2.

6.   **assert([a, c, d]).**

[a, c, d] is not a clause

retract(X)

'retract' is used for removing clauses from the database. It requires a single term as its argument, the term must be a valid and existing clause, otherwise the goal fails.

Executing the goal **retract(X)** causes the database to be searched for a clause which matches **X.** The goal succeeds if a match is found and the effect is that the matching clause is deleted from the database.

As with assert X must be bracketed if it contains the ':-' operator. Retract can be resatisfied on backtracking and will delete all the items for a clause if used with the fail goal, e.g.

> **cleanup:-retract(obsolete(N)), fail.**
> **cleanup.**

The cleanup predicate above, will retract an obsolete fact and then go on to the fail goal. The fail goal forces backtracking, retract tries to retract another obsolete fact, if it succeeds it goes on to the fail goal which forces backtracking again. If it fails then it goes on to the second cleanup clause, which always succeeds. The recursive version of the cleanup predicate is shown below.

> **cleanup:-retract(obsolete(N)), !, cleanup.**
> **cleanup.**

retractall(X)

retractall always succeeds, all clauses that can be matched with X will be deleted from the database. Executing the goal causes the database to be searched for clauses that match X. X must therefore be instantiated to a clause. The clause may have uninstantiated variables, but X itself may not be an uninstantiated variable.

The univ operator

X =.. L

The univ predicate is very useful for providing or obtaining arguments of a structure. Either X or L must be instantiated. L must be a list. If X is instantiated then L is the functor and arguments of X. For example

X = univ(arg1, no2, Arg3).

X =.. L

L = [univ, arg1, no2, Arg3].

If L is instantiated and X is not then X is the structure represented by L. For example

L = [this, is, an, example]

X =.. L

X = this(is, an, example).

?- append([a,b],[c,d],[a,b,c,d]) =..
            [append,[a,b],[c,d],[a,b,c,d]].

yes.

?- (a+B) =.. L.
L = [+,a, _21]

B = _21
.

We are going to write a predicate 'reveal' which takes a single argument and displays it in its internal representation. In some implementations this predicate is already defined, and called 'display'. It will be useful to see how the predicate is implemented (particularly when you come to implement the Expert system of chapter 14) so we will develop it here. We need two clauses. The first clause deals with an argument which is an atomic (an atom or a number). In some systems atomic is provided as a built in predicate. In other systems you may not have 'number' but you will definitely have 'integer'. If you do not have 'atomic' it is simply:

```
atomic(X)  :-
    atom(X);
    number(X).
```

if you do not have 'number' then atomic is:

```
atomic(X)  :-
    atom(X);
    integer(X).
```

The first clause of 'reveal' is quite straightforward, if the argument is an atom then write it as it is. In Prolog this is:

```
reveal(Atom)  :-
    atomic(Atom),
    !,
    write(Atom).
```

The second clause is a little trickier. What we need to do is to split the structure into its functor and arguments. This is best done using the 'univ' operator ('=..'). This is an infix operator provided by the Prolog system. 'univ' takes a structure and decomposes it into its *principal functor* and the arguments of the functor in the form of a list. The principal functor is the head of the list, and the tail of the list is the arguments to the functor. For example:

> on(cat, mat) =.. L.   L = [on, cat, mat]
> on(the(cat), the(mat)) L = [on,the(cat),the(mat)]

'univ' works in both directions either from a list to a structure or a structure to a list, e.g.

> Structure =.. [in, bat, cave]

> Structure = in(bat, cave)

We can therefore use 'univ' to provide the functor and arguments of a structure. In relation to our predicate 'reveal' we write the functor, then an opening bracket, then we can write the arguments. Hence the second clause of 'reveal' is:

```
reveal(Structure) :-
      Structure =.. [Functor | Args],
      write(Functor),
      write('('),
      write_args(Args),
      write(')').
```

We must now write a predicate 'write_args' which takes a single list of arguments (remember that the tail of a list is always a list) and prints out the arguments in turn. You must remember two things:

1. Each of the arguments could itself be a structure which needs 'revealing'.
2. After each argument we require a comma, except for the last one.

Again we require two rules to print the arguments, The first rule dealing with the case of there being only one item in the list (i.e. the last item):

```
write_args([X]) :-
    reveal(X).
```

The second clause deals with a list of more than one item, revealing the first item, writing a comma, and writing the rest of the arguments:

```
write_args([First | Rest]) :-
    reveal(First),
    write(','),
    write_args(Rest).
```

The whole program is therefore:

```
reveal(Atom) :-
    atomic(Atom),
    !,
    write(Atom).
reveal(Structure) :-
    Structure =.. [Functor | Args],
    write(Functor),
    write('('),
    write_args(Args),
    write(')').
```

```
write_args([X])  :-
      reveal(X).
write_args([First | Rest]) :-
      reveal(First),
      write(','),
      write_args(Rest).
```

Now try the following queries:

```
?- reveal(tom).
?- reveal(pals(tom, dick, harry)).
?- reveal([tom, dick, harry]).
?- reveal(3 * 4 - 5).
```

Name(Atom,List)

name relates an atom to the list of ascii codes comprising it. This is useful for finding the atom for some given characters, or the ascii characters for a given atom.   This is the standard implementation of name, below is the Prolog2 version of name.

```
?-  name(prolog,X).
```

X = [112, 114, 111, 108, 111, 103].

```
?-  name(carlton, "carlton").
```

yes.
```
?-  name(carlton,"masoud").
```

no.

```
?- name(X,[108,  111,  103,  111]).
```

X = logo

Name(Atom,String) Prolog2 implementation

name relates an atom to the string of ascii characters comprising it. When used in conjunction with the built in predicate **list** this predicate can be used to find the atom corresponding to a list of ascii characters, or the ascii characters corresponding to a given atom.

?- **name(prolog,X).**

X = "prolog".

?- **name(carlton,"carlton").**

yes.

?- **name(carlton,"masoud").**

no.

list(List, String) Prolog2 only

converts a string to a list of ascii characters or vice-versa.

functor

The built in predicate functor takes three arguments

functor(Structure, Functor, No_Args).

The predicate may be used in three ways.

1. If all three arguments are instantiated then functor returns true if the functor of the structure Structure is Functor and the number of arguments is equal to the variable No_Args. For example:

   ?- functor(animals(bat, cat, rat), animals, 3).

   yes.

   ?- functor(likes(people, democracy), animals, 2).

   no.

2. If the first argument is a variable then the other two arguments must be instantiated. The result will be that Structure will be a structure whose functor is that of Functor and the number of anonymous variables determined by the variable No_Args. If either of the other two arguments is uninstantiated then the predicate will fail.

   ?- functor(Structure, creation, 3).

   Structure = creation(_, _, _)

3. The third way that the predicate may be used is to have the first argument instantiated and the functor and/or the number of arguments may be uninstantiated variables. 'functor' will then generate the functor and number of arguments of the structure, e.g.

   ?- functor(colours(red,yellow,green,blue), Fun, Args).

   Fun = colours
   Args = 4

Arg

The built in predicate arg tends to be used in conjunction to either give values to variables in a structure or to find the values of arguments in a structure. 'arg' takes three arguments:

arg(Index, Structure, Value)

Index must not be an uninstantiated variable. **Structure** must be a structure and **Value** may be instantiated or uninstantiated. If it is instantiated then the argument indexed by **Index** must be the same as **Value** for the predicate to succeed. If the indexed argument is a variable then it will be instantiated to **Value**. If **Value** is uninstantiated then the result will be to match it with the indexed argument of **Structure**, the action of which will be to instantiate it if the indexed argument is not a variable, if it is a variable then they are made to share. For example:

?- arg(Var, friends(garfield, patrick), patrick).

no.

?- arg(1, ladies(lorraine, jenny, angela), Who).

Who = lorraine

?- arg(2, men(carlton, Pal, patrick), garfield).

Pal = garfield

?- functor(Primary, colours, 3),
       arg(1, Primary, red),
       arg(2, Primary, green),
       arg(3, Primary, blue).

Primary = colours(red, green, blue)

I am fully aware that some readers will take issue as to what the three primary colours are, nevertheless this is just an example.

Comparators

In order to facilitate the comparison of arguments in terms of both mathematical and logical equality Prolog provides the following comparators. All examples are given in terms of two variables X and Y.

X = Y   compares X and Y with the following results:

If X and Y are both atoms then the result is true if X and Y are the same atom.

?- **rat = rat.**   /* responds yes */

?- **cat = mat.**   /* responds no */

If either X or Y is a variable and the other argument an atom then the result will always be true, with the variable being instantiated to the atom.

?- **X = fat.**   /* yes, X instantiated to fat */

?- **fat = X.**   /* yes, X instantiated to fat */

If X and Y are both variables then X will be made to share with X

?- **X = Y, Y = cat, write(X).**

    cat
    X = cat
    Y = cat
    yes.

X == Y   Will only succeed if X and Y are either the same atom or sharing variables, in other words are X and Y the same thing?

X \= Y   not (X = Y) if X and Y are equal or can be made to share then the answer is negated. Will return true only if X and Y are both instantiated and to different atoms.

X \== Y   not (X == Y) Are X and Y different things or even different variables?

Exercises

1. Write a program that performs stack operations such that if we had two stacks **stack1** and **stack2**

	stack2(item6).
	stack2(item5).
	stack2(item4).
stack1(last)	**stack2(item3).**
stack1(second)	**stack2(item2).**
stack1(first)	**stack2(item1).**

the operations

  push(stack1,fourth)   give

```
stack1(fourth)
stack1(last)
stack1(second)
stack1(first)
```

and **pop(stack2,Item)** gives

Item = **item6** and a stack

```
stack2(item5).
stack2(item4).
stack2(item3).
stack2(item2).
stack2(item1).
```

2. Write another program **stacker** that performs stack operations on various stacks. The difference between this and the previous one is that stacker takes one argument which is a structure of the form

1.   **push(item).**
     pop(item).

2.   **push(stackn, item).**
     pop(stackn, item).

If the structure has only one argument then the operations are to be performed on a stack called **'pile',** otherwise the name of the stack will be the first argument, e.g.

   ?- stacker(push(next)).   /* adds item **next** to 'pile' */

pile(next)

   :

pile(bottom)

?- **stacker(pop(stack1,Top))**.

takes the top item off stack1 e.g.

Top = fourth

3. Write a predicate eman which takes an atom as a single argument and prints it out backwards, e.g.

?- **eman(notlrac)**.

carlton

yes.

CHAPTER 6

Arithmetic

Prolog allows the user to use arithmetic expressions which are evaluated by the built in predicate/operator 'is'. The expressions can be arbitrarily complex in the same way that expressions may be of arbitrary complexity in ordinary arithmetic. There is nothing unusual about the way that Prolog processes such arithmetic expressions. By declaring mathematical operators (see chapter 11 on declaring your own operators) Prolog allows the mathematical expressions to be written as they are written normally and not in the prefix notation that is more akin to Prolog syntax.

The usage of the is operator is in the following form:

?- **X is Y.**

Y must be a **structure** which can be evaluated and therefore must be an arithmetic expression. The result of the evaluation is compared to **X**. If **X** is already instantiated then the success of the **'is'** operation is based on the comparison. If **X** is uninstantiated then **X** is instantiated to the result.

The operators that can be used to build the right hand structures are

+   -   *   /

X + Y   An infix operator, the precedence of which varies from implementation to implementation.

The addition operator, when evaluated by **'is'** yields a result which is the numerical sum of its two arguments.

e.g.	result
a) 1 + 2	3
b) 2 + (1 + 2)	5
c) 2 + 3 + 4	9
d) (1 + 2) + (3 + 4)	10
e) 6 + V if V instantiated to (say) 7	13
else	goal fails

X - Y   An infix operator of equal precedence to '+'.

The subtraction operator, when evaluated using **'is'** the result is the numerical difference between the two arguments.

e.g.	result
a) 2 - 1	1
b) 2 - 4	-2
c) (8 + 2) - 6 + (3 - 8)	-1
d) 6 - V if V instantiated to 7	13
else if V uninstantiated	goal fails

X * Y   An infix operator of precedence less than '+' and '-'.

When evaluated by **'is'** its result is the numerical product of its two arguments.

X / Y   An infix operator of precedence equal to that of '*'.

When evaluated by 'is' its result is the numerical quotient of its two arguments.

	e.g.	**result**
a)	**3 / 2**	1.5
b)	**4 / 2**	2
c)	**8 / 4 * 2**	1
d)	**6 + 12 / 3 * 2**	3
e)	**6 + 19 / 3 * 6 - 2**	2.00805

X mod Y infix operator of precedence less than that of '*' and '/'.

When evaluated by the **'is'** operator, its result is the remainder that is generated by **X / Y** (X divided by Y)

	e.g.	**result**
a)	**3 mod 2**	1
b)	**5 mod 8**	5
c)	**7 * 2 mod 11**	3

Arithmetic comparators

X < Y   returns true if X is numerically less than Y, otherwise returns false.

X > Y   returns true if X is numerically greater than Y, otherwise returns false.

X =< Y   returns true if X is numerically less than or equal to Y, otherwise returns false.

X <= Y   returns true if X is numerically greater than or equal to Y, otherwise returns false.

The above four comparators do not evaluate their arguments first. The arguments are compared and the results are only guaranteed to work with numerical arguments. Characters, atoms and strings are not converted to ascii before comparison. The following examples all yield a "no" from the interpreter.

a < b	and	b < a.
'a' < 'b'	and	'b' < 'a'
apple < banana	and	banana < apple
"apple" < "banana"	and	"banana" < "apple"

Evaluate and compare

X =:= Y   evaluates both expressions X and Y returning true if they are equal, and false if they are different.

X =/= Y   evaluates both expressions X and Y returning true if they are not equal, returning false otherwise.

Factorial predicate

This example writes the factorial predicate. The factorial of 4 is 4 x 3 x 2 x 1 = 24. The predicate factorial takes 2 arguments, the number for which the factorial is sought as input, and output is the factorial of that number.

?- **factorial(4, X).**

X = 24
more y/n

The factorial of zero is 1, i.e.

?- **factorial(0,X).**

X = 1
more y/n

A general statement of the problem is:

If we need to find the factorial of N (i.e. N x N-1 x N-2 x N-3 ..
..1) then find the factorial of N-1 and multiply this intermediate
result by N.

The solution is to first write the simple fact that the factorial
of zero is one.

factorial(0, 1).

The next thing to do is to code the general rule. This involves
three steps

1. find N - 1 (lets call it M)
2. find the factorial of M (i.e. N-1, call this X)
3. multiply the factorial of N-1 (i.e. X) by N to give the
   result

This second rule in Prolog is:

factorial(N,Result) :-
        M is N - 1,
        factorial(M, X),
        Result is N * X.

The whole predicate then, is:

factorial(0, 1).
factorial(N, Result) :-
    M is N - 1,
    factorial(M, X),
    Result is N * X.

What happens if the two rules are reversed ?

What happens if we ask ?

        ?- factorial(-3, N).

Summary

Expression	Associativity	Precedence	result
X + Y	y f x	31 or 500	Sum of X + Y
X - Y	y f x	31 or 500	Result of X minus Y
X * Y	y f x	21 or 400	Product of X and Y
X / Y	y f x	21 or 400	Integer quotient of X divided by Y
X mod Y	x f x	11 or 300	Integer remainder of X divided by Y
X div Y	y f x	21	Integer quotient of X divided by Y

Exercises

1. Write a predicate **count** that counts the number of items in a list. **count** takes two arguments, the first argument being the list, the second argument the number of elements in that list.

2. Write a predicate triangle which finds the number of balls in a triangle of base N. For example:

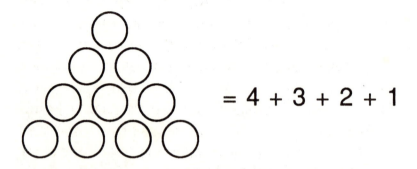

$$= 4 + 3 + 2 + 1$$

Express the solution in English first. In other words specify the terminating condition and then the general continuation condition.

CHAPTER 7

Recursion

The most natural and efficient way of producing solutions on a computer is by using recursion. Most programs are executed using a stack, each call to a procedure invokes another layer on the stack. The stack mechanism is recursive and executes programs quite simply. In addition to the way in which programs are executed many concepts are recursive in nature, that is, can be defined in terms of themselves. Consider for example an integer, an integer is a digit followed by an integer, which is a digit followed by another integer and so on. We could then use this precise definition to prove that any number was in fact an integer. First we look at the first character and check to see if it is in fact a digit, then we look at the next digit and check to see if that is a digit until the string of characters has been exhausted.

In any recursive approach to solving a problem, it is important that upon each successive level of recursion the problem is decomposed in such a way that we are either closer to a solution, or we approach a point where the problem cannot be decomposed any further. If this decomposition does not take place, or we do not approach the solution then we are likely to fall into an infinite loop.

We have already seen the factorial predicate, which is in fact recursive. In this chapter we will develop a recursive solution from a non-recursive solution. In reality many problems, in Prolog, cannot be solved except by using recursive definitions. Consider the following two rules:

1. An item is a list if it is the empty list.
2. An item is a list if you can take its head element, and its tail is

a list.

one possible program is

```
islist([]).
islist([H | T]) :- restlist(T).

restlist([]).
restlist([H | T]) :- islist(T).
```

If we call

```
?- islist([]).
```

the system responds:

```
yes.
```

If we try:

```
?- islist(a, b).
```

the system responds:

```
no.
```

If we try:

```
?- islist(a).
```

the system responds:

```
no.
```

if we try:

   ?- **islist([i, j]).**

a call would be made, finding a match with the second **islist** clause, i.e.

level 1

   islist([H | T]) :- restlist(T).

   with **H = i**   and   **T = [j]**

   islist([i, j]) :- restlist([j]).

   i.e. **[i, j]** is a list if **restlist([j]).**

N.B.

   [j] is really **[j, []]**

   j   []

A call is then made by the system to search for:

   restlist([j]).

level 2

the second **restlist** clause matches, i.e.

   restlist([H | T]) :- islist(T).

with **H = j** and **T = []**, that is:

restlist([j]) :- islist([]).

In other words, **restlist([j])** is true if **islist([])**

level 3

a call is made to **islist** with **T** instantiated to **[]**

islist([])

matches the first **islist** clause therefore level 3 succeeds, causing

restlist([j]) :- islist([]).   **-- level 2**

to succeed which causes

islist([i,j]) :- restlist([j])   **-- level 1**

to succeed which causes the original goal

islist([i,j]) to succeed

the system then responds

yes.

You can see that the two predicates are **recursive** or more correctly **mutually recursive**. In Prolog this is perfectly reasonable. But why not have:

islist([]).
islist([H | T]) :- islist(T).

this makes **islist** a recursive predicate, this is also perfectly reasonable. In English these two rules say that

1. Something is a list if it is the empty list

2. Something is a list if after removing its head element its tail is a list.

The **islist** program is now only two lines long! This is one of the advantages of using recursive predicates, all our code is extremely succinct.

Make sure that you understand what is going on here, because your appreciation of Prolog is dependent upon your understanding of recursion. To write Prolog programs effectively you **must** be able to write recursively, read recursively, think recursively ?

Example

1. ?- **islist([x, y, z]).**

really [x, y, z, []]

a match is made with the second **islist** clause with

H = x and **T = [y, z]**

so the original query is true if (:-) **islist(T)** is true. As **T** is instantiated to **[y, z]** the system tries to find:

islist([y, z]).

2. The second call is **islist([y, z])** again the second clause matches this time with

H = y and **T = [z]**

The second call is true if **islist(T)** is true and **T** is instantiated to [z]. The system tries to find

islist([z]).

3. The search of the database again picks up the second **islist** clause, with

H = z and **T = []**

The clause is true if **islist(T)** is true **T** being instantiated to [] (the empty list). Therefore the system tries to find

islist([]).

4. The call **islist([])** matches the first islist clause which causes the third call to succeed, which in turn causes the second call to succeed, which in turn causes the first call to succeed. An explanation could be given in this manner: [x, y, z] is a list because the [y, z] is a list. [y, z] is a list because [z] is a list. [z] is a list because [] is a list. [] is a list because we have found the fact **islist([])** in the database.

?- **islist([x, y, z]).**

The system then responds

yes.

Consider the following recursive predicate, the rules of which can be stated in English as follows:

1. Appending the empty list to any list produces the same list. This is the boundary condition.

2. Appending two lists can be done by taking the head item of the first list, and making it the head of the list whose tail is the result of appending the tail of the first list with the second list.

append([], L, L).
append(List1, List2, List3) :-
      List1 = [Head | Tail],   /* take the head of the first list */
      append(Tail, List2, Result), /* append tail to 2nd list */
      List3 = [Head | Result]. /* new tail is result of append */

The predicate can be optimised by letting the pattern matcher do the work for us in the head of the second clause, i.e.

append([Head | Tail], List2, [Head | Result]) :-
      append(Tail, List2, Result).

Suppose we want to append the following two lists: [v, w] [x, y, z], the call

      ?- append([v, w], [x, y, z], L).

returns **L = [v, w, x, y, z]**

We will have a look at the execution of this predicate for a greater appreciation of what can be done using recursive predicates. Consider the call

1. append([a, b], [c, d, e], L).

The system tries to find a match in the database, and finds the second **append** clause i.e.

append([Head | Tail], List2, [Head | Result]) :-
    append(Tail, List2, Result).

with

Head = a   Tail = [b]   List2 = [c, d, e]   Result = ?

The original **L** in the query is instantiated to **[a | Z]**

append([a, b], [c, d, e], L) is therefore true if

append([b], [c, d, e], Result) is true.

2. append([b], [c, d, e], Result) causes a search of the database which finds a match with the second append clause, with

Head = b   Tail = []   List2 = [c, d, e]   Result = ??

This **Result** is **not** the same as the **Result** at level 1, so to avoid confusion we will call it **Result$_2$**

Result is instantiated to **[b | Result$_2$]**

append([b], [c, d, e], Result) is therefore true if

append([], [c, d, e], Result$_2$) is true.

3. append([], [c, d, e], Result₂) causes a search of the
database, and finds a match with the first **append** clause, i.e.

append([], L, L).   where **L = [c, d, e]**

Result₂ is instantiated to **L** (argument 3)
L is instantiated to **[c, d, e]** (argument 2)

The level 3 call succeeds with **Result₂ = [c, d, e]**

2. Result   = [b | Result₂]   **Result₂ = [c, d, e]**

  therefore   **Result = [b, c, d, e]**

1. L = [a | Result]   therefore **L = [a, b, c, d, e]**

system therefore responds

L = [a, b, c, d, e]

Review

level   call   variables

top   **append([a, b], [c, d, e], L)   L = ?**

match causes the following instantiations **Head = a**
                                          Tail = [b]
                                          List2 = [c, d, e]
                                          Result = ?
                                          L = [a | Result]

1.   append([b], [c, d, e], Result)

match creates another set of variables   **Head = b**
                                           Tail = []
                                           List2 = [c, d, e]
                                           Result = ??

the **Result** in the level 1 call becomes   **Result = [b | Result]**
the **L** in the top level becomes   **L = [a | [b | Result]]**
        i.e.   **L = [a, b | Result]**

2.   append([], [c, d, e], Result)

matches the first append clause   **L = [c, d, e]**

                                            Result = L
therefore   **Result = [c, d, e]**
Result in level 1   **Result = [b | c, d, e]**
L in top level   **L = [a | b, c, d, e]**

Summary

When writing recursive predicates care must be taken to ensure termination. A 'boundary condition' must be identified and used to terminate the recursion.

The ordering of goals is also a crucial consideration. For example consider the ancestor predicate, it could be rewritten:

ancestor(X, Y) :- ancestor(Z, Y), parent(X, Z).
ancestor(X, Y) :- parent(X, Y).

If the ancestors of everyone who ever lived were in the database then the call

ancestor(adam, carlton)

would take centuries finding all the ancestors of everyone that ever lived !

Exercises

1. Using the royal database, write a predicate **parent** such that:

> X is a **parent** of Y if
> > X is the father of Y.

OR

> X is a **parent** of Y if
> > X is the mother of Y.

Write a predicate ancester (ancester has been deliberately misspelt because Prolog2 has a built in predicate called ancestor) such that:

> X is an **ancester** of Y if
> > X is the parent of Y.

OR

> X is the **ancester** of Y if
> > X is the parent of Z and
> > Z is the **ancester** of Y.

What happens if the the parent and ancester goals are reversed in the second ancester clause ?

How is the efficiency of the execution affected if the two clauses are reversed ?

2. Write a predicate **last**, which takes two arguments the first is the list, the second is the last item in the list. For example:

>?- **last([a, b, c], L).**

L = c

>?- **last([c, b, a], a).**

yes.

>?- **last([a, b, c], d).**

no.

terminating condition

>if we have a list with one element then that element is the last one.

continuation condition

>if we want to find the last item in a list find the last item in the tail of the list.

Try out your predicate using the following queries

a) **last([d, o, g], L).**

b) **last([dog, cat, pig], pig).**

c) **last(frog, [pig, dog]).**

3. Write a predicate **reverse** that reverses a list. Reverse takes

two arguments. The first is the list to be reversed the second is the reverse of the first.

test it with:

a) **reverse([a, b, c], P).**

b) **reverse([p, q, r], [r, q, p]).**

c) **reverse(L, [z, y, x, w]).**

4.   Write a recursive predicate **member** that takes two arguments. The first argument is an atom the second argument is a list. **Member** returns **true** if the element is a member of the list.

What happens with the following queries?

a) **member(a, [a, b, d]).**

b) **member(c, [e, g, c]).**

c) **member(d, [i, j, k]).**

5. Write a predicate **shuffle**, that shuffles two lists (interleaving items). Shuffle takes 3 arguments, the two lists, and the interleaved version of the two lists.

For example

a) **shuffle([a, c, e], [b, d], A).**

    returns

A = [a, b, c, d, e]

b) **shuffle([], [t, u, r, t, l, e], L).**

   returns

L = [t, u, r, t, l, e]

c) **shuffle([t, u, r, t, l,.e], [], L).**

   returns

L = [t, u, r, t, l, e]

d) **shuffle([i, s, a, t, a, i, n], [n, t, n, i, t, o], L).**

   returns

L = [i, n, s, t, a, n, t, i, a, t, i, o, n]

CHAPTER 8

Efficient Prolog Programming

The execution efficiency of Prolog programs can be enhanced by using cuts at boundary conditions and secondly, by making all solutions tail recursive. Consider for example the predicates **member**, **append** and **reverse**.

```
member(Item, [Item | _]).
member(Item, [_ | Tail]) :- member(Item, Tail).

append([], L, L).
append([Head | List1], List2, [Head | List3]) :-
    append(List1, List2, List3).

reverse([], []).
reverse([H | T], Z):-
    reverse(T, L),
    append(L, [H], Z).
```

All three predicates can be optimised. The predicate member, if not being used to generate members of a list; or the predicate append if not being used to generate pairs of lists from a list provided as the third argument can be optimised by changing the boundary condition, to having a single subgoal which is a cut. That is:

```
member(Item, [Item | _]) :- !.
member(Item, [_ | Tail]) :- member(Item, Tail).
```

```
append([], L, L) :- !.
append([Head | List1], List2, [Head | List3]) :-
    append(List1, List2, List3).
```

The reason that this is more efficient is that when Prolog reaches the boundary condition, it remembers that there is an alternative clause that could potentially match. During reverse there are several calls to append, each call needs to be remembered so that if backtracking takes place the interpreter is able to return to try the second append clause. By cutting off the alternative at the boundary condition, we do not need to remember the alternative way of satisfying **append**. Using a cut whenever possible, significantly reduces the search space and allows more levels of recursion to be explored.

The predicate **append** may be optimised by changing the order of the clauses. Every time the execution recurses, a check is made to see if the first argument is the empty list. This test could be made implicitly by changing the order of the clauses. If we repeatedly take the head and tail of the first argument, then eventually when the list is empty, the head and tail will fail to match and the terminating condition will match trivially. The final version of **append** is therefore:

```
append([Head | List1], List2, [Head | List3]) :-
    append(List1, List2, List3).
append([], L, L).
```

In Prolog, when a clause executes, a frame is placed on the stack, which represents the state of the execution environment at the time of the call. Frame information includes pointers to the next clause should this one fail. The variable instantiations are recorded so that when backtracking variables will be uninstantiated in the appropriate places. The size of the stack depends largely upon the number of variables in the head of the clause, and whether there are alternatives to the clause. That is, whether the frame is a choice frame or a non-choice frame.

The interpreter utilises the following workspace during the execution of a clause:

> ✐ A local stack that records all the goals invoked by the clause.

> ✐ A global stack for copying variable instantiations.

> ✐ A trail of variable addresses to be cleared on backtracking.

The second way of making predicates more efficient is by making them *tail recursive*. We will use the reverse predicate to illustrate this point. You will notice that when reversing a list, when a return is made to each level of recursion the result has to be appended to the head of the list at that level. The implications are that at each recursive call we have to store the next subgoals (in this case just the single append goal) on the stack. Eventually when we get to the bottom level of recursion, we have n append goals on the stack. The variables at each level will also need to be recorded. If we change the order of the append and reverse subgoals we have a better scenario:

```
reverse([], []).
reverse([H | T], Z):-
      append(L, [H], Z),
      reverse(T, L).
```

At each recursive call there are no goals to perform on the way out. All that happens is that we have a series of instantiations to make as we reach the last element of the list. We do not need to keep any goals on the stack. This is what is known as a tail recursive routine, the recursive call is the last in the list of subgoals. More recent implementations will have a feature called tail recursion optimisation. ***Tail recursion optimisation*** takes the recursive call and overwrites the head goal on the stack.

```
head(A, B, C):-
    subgoal1(A, X),
    subgoal2(B, Y),
        :
        :
    subgoaln(X, Y, C).
```

The conditions under which tail recursion (if supported) optimisation apply are:

☞ there must be no choice points, i.e. nowhere to backtrack to between the head goal and the tail goal. A choice point is a resatisfiable goal.

☞ All the variables in the tail goal must either share with another variable in the subgoals, or must appear in the head of the clause.

☞ A cut must not follow the tail goal.

head(A, B, C) must have no alternative clauses for reduction left. The subgoals must be deterministic, i.e. subgoal1, subgoal2, subgoal$_{n-1}$ cannot be resatisfied, and cannot generate alternative solutions. Some examples may clarify the point here.

```
head :-
    resatisfiable,        /* can be resatisfied */
    head.
```

```
head :-
    (goal ; goal2),          /* can backtrack into it */
    head.
```

Both of the above examples cannot be tail recursion optimised. The following however can be.

```
head :- cutgoal,         /* cut and cannot be resatisfied */
head.

goal(X, Z) :-
    subgoal1(Y),
        :
        :
    !,                   /* the cut prevents backtracking */
    goal(Y, Z).
```

The simplest way to ensure that tail recursion optimisation conditions apply is to cut the penultimate goal as illustrated with the last example.

Tail recursion optimisation is implemented by comparing backtracking related information for head clause and subgoal$_n$. Clause indexing detects which clauses are applicable to reduction before matching. Typically, indexing is done on the **type** and **value** of the **first** argument. For example:

```
append([Head | List1], List2, [Head | List3]) :-
    append(List1, List2, List3).
append([], L, L).
```

If appending two complete lists by the time we hit the recursive goal, if clauses are indexed then we know that backtracking cannot take place successfully, and therefore conditions for tail recursion optimisation hold.

Extra arguments for greater efficiency

The predicate **reverse** can be optimised even further. The reversed list is built up on the way back up the levels of recursion but if we could somehow record the reversed list so far and forget about everything else, then that would be even more efficient. The approach is to use an extra argument which keeps a copy of the reversed list so far, and passes it down to each recursive call of **reverse**.

```
reverse([], []).
reverse(L, R) :- reverse(L, [], R).

reverse([], Sofar, Sofar).
reverse([Head | Tail], Sofar, Reversed) :-
    reverse(Tail, [Head | Sofar], Reversed).
```

Summary

To make Prolog code more efficient

♪   cut boundary condition

♪   add extra aguments

♪   do all processing on the way down through recursive levels, if possible

♪   use tail recursion optimisation (if available)

Exercise

1.   Write a tail recursive version of the factorial predicate, that uses an extra variable to keep a copy of the factorial sofar.

Part Two:

Projects

CHAPTER 9

Prolog as a Production System

In this chapter we shall attempt to construct a very simple Expert system using Prolog. Interested readers should also consult Clark and McCabe (1982) for a successful exposition of Prolog as an Expert System construction tool, in which they not only go further than our example, but also remain true to Prolog's 'logical' view of the world. Here we use Prolog as if it were a production system.

Prolog provides us with a database in which we can accommodate production rules in the form:

> CONCLUSION if
> > PRECONDITION1 and
> > PRECONDITION2

In the 'logical' interpretation of Prolog this means:

> To prove CONCLUSION
> > prove PRECONDITION1 and
> > prove PRECONDITION2

The Prolog syntax for all this is simple, ':-' stands for 'if', and ',' stands for 'and'. Each production is terminated with a full stop.

If there are two or more ways of proving a conclusion, we can write each of these as an independent rule. Prolog would try the first rule first. Failing that it would try successive rules until either one succeeds or all fail. Prolog also enables us to accommodate facts (as rules with no preconditions) which are always true.

Whether a rule is applicable is determined by pattern matching. The user's query is matched against the conclusion part of the rules in the current database. If the matching process succeeds it also instantiates all the variables occurring within the rule to specific matching values found in the query. These values will then be used only by the precondition part of the same rule. The precondition part can be any procedure and it is evaluated only if the match succeeds and the rule is selected by the control mechanism.

The precondition parts of a selected rule, themselves act as queries to be proved. The control mechanism provided by Prolog is what is known as depth first search, or backward chaining. The order of the appearance of facts and rules in the database guides this control process. We start at the top and work our way down. This general structure is illustrated in Figure 9.1.

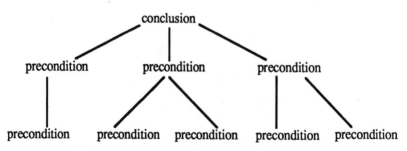

Fig. 9.1 The structure of a decision tree

An expert system

A large number of expert systems are implemented as a set of production rules. When the system starts, a simple rule is invoked which gathers some initial information about the particular case which the user is dealing with, and adds the information to the database. From then on the system follows a basic 'select a rule to apply its associated preconditions', keep doing this until you cannot go any further! The centralised database is the focus of all activity, and the programmer has to produce essentially complex control strategies to ensure that the so-very-possible anarchy in the system is controlled towards a successful conclusion.

The great bulk of the database is made up of rules which are invoked by pattern matching with features of the case environment and which can be added to, modified or deleted by the user. A database of this type is known as a 'knowledge base'.

A simple expert system on animal discrimination (as in Winston and Horn, 1980) would be as follows.

Note that we have numbered each production rule in order to make the exposition of the ideas simple. Prolog does not, however, require any numbering of the rules or facts in the database. You should not type these numbers if you type the program into your computer.

1.1.0	it_is_a(cheetah) :-
1.1.1	it_is(mammal),
2	it_is(carnivore),
3	has(tawny_colour),
4	has(dark_spots).

1.2.0	it_is_a(tiger) :-
1.2.1	it_is(mammal),
2	it_is(carnivore),
3	has(tawny_colour),
4	has(dark_stripes).

1.3.0	it_is_a(giraffe) :-

```
1.3.1              it_is(ungulate),
   2               has(long_neck),
   3               has(long_legs),
   4               has(dark_spots).


1.4.0     it_is_a(zebra) :-
1.4.1              it_is(ungulate),
   2               has(black_stripes).


1.5.0     it_is_a(ostrich) :-
1.5.1              it_is(bird),
   2               does(not_fly),
   3               has(long_neck),
   4               has(long_legs),
   5               has(black_and_white_colour).


1.6.0     it_is_a(penguin) :-
1.6.1              it_is(bird),
   2               does(not_fly),
   3               does(swim),
   4               has(black_and_white_colour).


1.7.0     it_is_a(albatross) :-
1.7.1              it_is(bird),
   2               does(fly_well).
```

We also need the following:

```
2.1.0     it_is(mammal) :-
2.1.1              has(hair).


2.2.0     it_is(mammal) :-
2.2.1              does(give_milk).
```

These two definitions of mammal indicate that it either has hair OR gives milk. Either of these qualities would be sufficient in order for something to be a mammal.

```
2.3.0        it_is(bird) :-
2.3.1                has(feathers).


2.4.0        it_is(bird) :-
2.4.1                does(fly),
     2               does(lay_eggs).


2.5.0        it_is(carnivore) :-
2.5.1                does(eat_meat).


2.6.0        it_is(carnivore) :-
2.6.1                has(pointed_teeth),
     2               has(claws),
     3               has(forward_eyes).


2.7.0        it_is(ungulate) :-
2.7.1                it_is(mammal),
     2               has(hoofs).


2.8.0        it_is(ungulate) :-
2.8.1                it_is(mammal),
     2               does(chew_cud).
```

As we said earlier, in an expert system, initially the database would be free of any facts about the current situation. Therefore we need a simple conversational section in our program to gather information from the user.

```
3.1.0        has(Y) :-
3.1.1             write(" has it got "),
    2             write(Y), nl,
    3             read(R),
    4             positive(R),
    5             asserta(has(Y)).
```

The 'nl' on line 3.1.2 is one of Prolog's built in predicates which results in a new line being printed out.

```
4.1.0        does(Y) :-
4.1.1             write(" does it "),
    2             write(Y),nl,
    3             read(R),
    4             positive(R),
    5             asserta(does(Y)).

5.1.0        positive(yes).

5.2.0        positive(y).
```

We finally need a definition of the overall task:

```
6.1.0        run:-
6.1.1             it_is_a(Y),
    2             write(" I think it is a "),
    3             write(Y), nl, nl.

6.2.0        run :-
6.2.1             write(" I don't know what your animal is "),nl.
```

All the user needs to do is type run and the system will do the rest.

How does Prolog work it all out?

Due to the control mechanism provided by Prolog, the result would be a search through the database for the meaning of 'run'. This is provided by line 6.1.0. In order to satisfy the request to 'run' by the user, Prolog then has to prove what appears under 6.1.0 to 6.1.3. The system starts from the top, attempting 6.1.1 first. This leads to another search in the database, taking us to 1.1.0 where Y is instantiated to 'cheetah' and control passes to 1.1.1 in order to prove 'it_is(mammal)', another search in the database takes us to 2.1.0 looking for 'mammal'. 2.1.0 has one precondition: 'has(hair)'. The next search through the database leads us to 3.1.0. Precondition 3.1.1 is satisfied by a built in predicate **write** resulting in the message "has it got " being printed out at the users terminal. Precondition 3.1.2 prints out "mammal" followed by a new line. Precondition 3.1.3 is also satisfied by a built in predicate which reads the user's input and instantiates R with it.

Now the user has the first question on the terminal:

has it got hair

Let us be positive to start with and say 'yes'. This instantiates R with 'yes'. Precondition 3.1.4 takes us back to another search of the database, taking us to 5.1.0. This results in a successful match with no preconditions to satisfy. Precondition 3.1.5 utilises another built in predicate which asserts a new fact to the database before other similar facts. In this case 'has(hair)' will be added just before 3.1.0. The system has collected its first fact about the animal in question.

We can go back and see what other preconditions at a higher level have not been checked yet. Prolog's control mechanism has put all of the previously unattended preconditions on a stack, following a last-in first-out strategy, leading us to a satisfaction of 2.1.0, which in turn leads us back to 1.1.1. We are now ready to try 1.1.2.

Precondition 1.1.2 takes us to 2.5.0 which follows the same steps above and which leads to the following being printed at the user's terminal:

does it eat_meat

Let us say what happens if we answer in the negative and say 'no', well 4.1.0 will lead to a search of the database looking for 'positive(no)'; reaching the end of the database without success, and therefore will be considered as a failure by the Prolog system, consequently 4.1.0 also fails since it fails to satisfy one of its preconditions. 2.5.0 therefore, will also fail.

It should be noted however, that when a precondition has failed and we are backtracking to the condition which called it, we will try other possible alternatives, if they are available. In this case this leads to 2.6.0 being attempted and the question:

has it got pointed_teeth

Let us still be negative and say 'no'. This will lead to a failure of 1.1.2. Prolog will try another alternative to 1.2.1 before giving up on 1.2.0. A new version of 1.2.1 will lead to 2.2.0 which produces the question:

does it give_milk

Let us say 'yes', thereby causing 1.2.1 to succeed. This means that we are now ready to try to go forward: 'maybe things further away have changed now that we have another success' will be Prolog's philosophy. Trying 1.2.2 reproduces a question that we have already been asked:

does it eat_meat

This is due to the fact that our program is not sophisticated enough to remember negative facts in the same way that it remembers positive ones. The next chapter will present an improved version which remedies this and other problems with the above program. To be consistent however, let us try the alternative and say 'no' again ! This leads to 1.2.2 failing. As we have now tried all the alternatives to 1.2.1, we have 1.1.0 failing too. Well, all that we have done is fail to prove that the animal in question is a cheetah, having learnt that it has hair !

You can guess that we will be trying to prove that it is a tiger next and so on in the order of the rules presented until we finally succeed, depending upon the order of the users positive and negative answers.

CHAPTER 10

An Expert System

expert system

The simple program for the discrimination of animals presented in the last chapter leaves a lot to be desired. Interaction with it becomes rather frustrating as it asks the same questions over and over again.

has it got hair	yes
does it eat_meat	no
has it got pointed_teeth	no
does it give milk	no
(has hair succeeds since it is in the database)	
does it eat_meat	no
has it got pointed teeth	no

Why does it keep asking about the pointed_teeth and eat_meat !

One of the shortcomings of the system as we have written it, is that although it notes the positive replies and adds the corresponding fact to the database it does not do the same with negative replies.

The first reaction would be to attempt to modify the 'does' and 'has' definitions to:

```
3.1.0       has(Y) :-
3.1.1               write(" has it got "),
      2               write(Y),nl,
      3               read(R),
      4               negative(R),
      5               asserta(has_not(Y) :- !).
```

```
4.1.0        does(Y) :-
4.1.1               write(" does it "),
   2                write(Y),nl,
   3                read(R),
   4                negative(R),
   5                asserta(does_not(Y) :- !).
```

The above solution introduces a major error into the discrimination process in the case of the penguin which in its definition has the attribute: 'does(not_fly)'. The two pieces of information 'does_not(fly)' and 'does(not_fly)' are not considered to be the same by Prolog as their patterns do not match. Therefore we would not obtain a satisfactory solution.

A more radical solution would be to devise a set of positive and negative predicates in the definitions of the animals.

One solution would be to go back and modify the definition of penguin to the form 'does_not(fly)' which in turn would require a set of rules for gathering information for 'does_not' and possibly 'has_not' in a similar way to the 'does' and 'has' arguments in a more general relation called 'positive', and in their negative form arguments of a relation called 'negative'.

```
        it_is_a(cheetah) :-
               it_is(mammal),
               it_is(carnivore),
               positive(has, tawny_colour),
               positive(has, dark_spots).

        it_is_a(tiger) :-
               it_is(mammal),
               it_is(carnivore),
               positive(has, tawny_colour),
               positive(has, dark_stripes).
```

```
it_is_a(giraffe) :-
        it_is(ungulate),
        positive(has, long_neck),
        positive(has, long_legs),
        positive(has, dark_spots).

it_is_a(zebra) :-
        it_is(ungulate),
        positive(has, black_stripes).

it_is_a(ostrich) :-
        it_is(bird),
        negative(does, fly),
        positive(has, long_neck),
        positive(has, long_legs),
        positive(has, black_and_white_colour).

it_is_a(penguin) :-
        it_is(bird),
        negative(does, fly),
        positive(does, swim),
        positive(has, black_and_white_colour).

it_is_a(albatross) :-
        it_is(bird),
        positive(does, fly_well).

it_is(mammal) :-
        positive(has, hair).
it_is(mammal) :-
        positive(does, give_milk).
it_is(bird) :-
        positive(has, feathers).
```

```
it_is(bird) :-
        positive(does, fly),
        positive(does, lay_eggs).

it_is(carnivore) :-
        positive(does, eat_meat).
it_is(carnivore) :-
        positive(has, pointed_teeth),
        positive(has, claws),
        positive(has, forward_eyes).

it_is(ungulate) :-
        it_is(mammal),
        positive(has, hoofs).
it_is(ungulate) :-
        it_is(mammal),
        positive(does, chew_cud).
```

We would then also need:

```
positive(X, Y) :-
        pos_fact(X, Y), !.
positive(X, Y) :-
        neg_fact(X, Y), !, fail.
positive(X, Y) :-
        ask(X, Y, R),
        yes_check(R).

negative(X, Y) :-
        neg_fact(X, Y), !.
negative(X, Y) :-
        pos_fact(X, Y), !, fail.
negative(X, Y) :-
        ask(X, Y, R),
        no_check(R).
```

```
yes_check(yes).

no_check(no).

ask(X, Y, R) :-
        write(X),
        write(" it "),
        write(Y),
        read(R),
        remember(R, X, Y).

remember(yes, X, Y) :-
        asserta(pos_fact(X, Y)).
remember(no, X, Y) :-
        asserta(neg_fact(X,Y)).

run:-
        it_is_a(Y),
        write(" I think it is a "),
        write(Y), nl, nl.
run:-
    write(" I don't know what your animal is "), nl.
```

CHAPTER 11

Operators

At this point in the book you should know that if you wanted to represent the relation:

    john likes mary

you would type it in as a Prolog fact:

    likes(john, mary)

In arithmetic however when we want to say:

    2 * 3

we do not need to translate it into the Prolog representation, i.e.

    *(2, 3)

The ability to write arithmetic expressions in a way which is intelligible to us, is made possible by the ability to declare operators. The fact 'john likes mary' would normally give a syntax error, but if we declare 'likes' to be an infix operator, then we can write:

    john likes mary   and   likes(john, mary)

and Prolog is unable to distinguish between the two.

The term 'operator' is a little misleading because Prolog operators do not in reality operate on anything. They are merely a notational convenience, a bit of 'syntactic sugar' that can be sprinkled on our programs to make them easier to read. As a consequence the user is able to understand expressions that the system translates for internal representation.

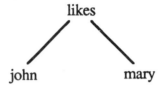

Here 'likes' is an infix operator, it is positioned between its arguments. The arguments are the atoms 'john' and 'mary'. By definition, Prolog atoms have a precedence of zero. In order for 'likes' to bind its arguments together it must have a precedence greater than that of its arguments (it can have a precedence equal to that of its arguments, this will be explained later in this chapter). It is not possible to have arguments of greater precedence than the operator.

To declare an operator

The built in predicate 'op' allows you to declare operators, 'op' takes three arguments:

op(precedence, associativity, operator).

If you enter:

op(1, xfx, likes)

in response to the '?-' prompt, and type (see chapter 6 for details of 'reveal'):

reveal(john likes mary).

We get:

likes(john, mary)

This means that whenever we type:

john likes mary   or   P likes Q

Prolog translates it into the internal representation. We could also define 'likes' as:

op(500, yfx, likes).
or   op(1200, xfy, likes).

The precedence is irrelevant as long as it is greater than its arguments (zero in this example) and not in excess of the permitted maximum (implementation dependent).

N.B. Operator declarations in a file must each be preceded by the prompt ('?-' on most systems).

Suppose that we wanted to to be able to represent the structure:

miss_piggy likes kermit and fozzy_bear.

Then we need to define as operators 'likes' and 'and'. In order to decide which of the words need to be declared as operators it is always a good idea to draw the structures out (rather like a parse tree in natural language parsing). For example:

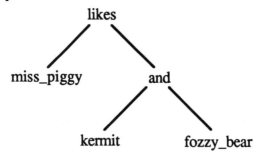

After we have drawn the tree there are two things to do:

1. Decide on the operator precedences.
2. Decide on the associativity of the operators.

Operator precedence

In the same way that arithmetic operators have a precedence which determines the order in which calculations are done, in Prolog operators also have a precedence to determine which arguments the operator takes. The way in which operator precedence is designated is fairly arbitrary. The only rule is the higher the operator in the tree the higher the precedence it must have. In assigning operator precedences we therefore start at the top and work down:

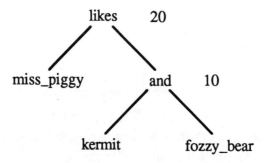

remembering that Prolog operators are deemed to have a

precedence of zero.

Operator associativity

Operator associativity is a little more difficult to decide. An infix operator can have one of three associativities:

    xfx   xfy   yfx

The 'f' stands for functor (or the operator), 'x' and 'y' stand for the position of the arguments. The fact that 'f' appears between the arguments indicates that it is an infix operator. If the same operator does not appear underneath itself in the tree, then you only ever need to use the 'xfx' associativity. If, however, the same operator appears in one of its subtrees (i.e. in one of the arguments) then you will have to use either 'yfx' or 'xfy' depending on whether it appears in the left or right subtree respectively. For example the sentence:

john likes mary and mary likes john.

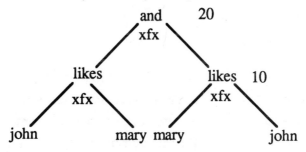

The operator declarations are:

    op(20, xfx, and).
    op(10, xfx, likes).

Although likes appears twice it does not appear underneath itself. We can therefore use 'xfx' to declare its associativity. It is now possible to type:

?- **reveal(john likes mary and mary likes john).**

to which reveal produces:

and(likes(john, mary), likes(mary, john)).

We could, however, represent 'john likes mary and mary likes john' in the following way:

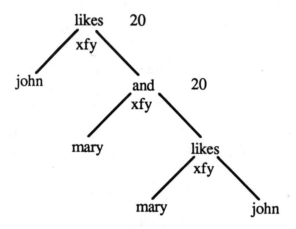

The precedence of 'likes' must remain the same throughout the tree, therefore whatever precedence and associativity we assign at an operator at one point in the tree must remain the same at every other point in the tree that the operator occurs. We can no longer use 'xfx' because an 'x' in an argument's position indicates that the argument in this position has a lower precedence than the operator. In this structure we need an operator with an equal precedence and so we use a 'y'. A 'y' in an argument's position indicates that the argument in this position has a lower or equal precedence to the operator.

You can see that such a representation of the sentence 'john likes mary and mary likes john' is not as clear as the previous one. It also makes it more difficult to allocate the operator associativities.

Why is an associativity of 'yfy' not allowed?

The reason for this restriction can best be illustrated by an example. Take, for instance, the sentence:

red and yellow and pink and green.

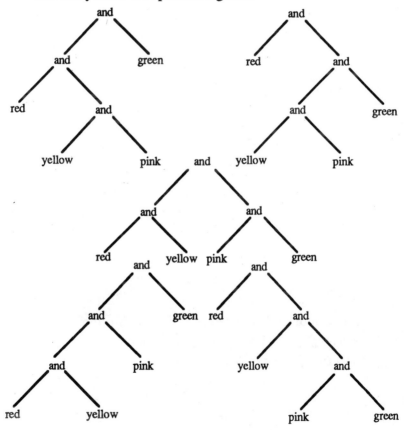

If 'and' were allowed to have an associativity of 'yfy' then the sentence could have any of the above five structures.

As another example (from a mathematical point of view), if we declared the minus sign as having an associativity of 'yfy', then would the expression:

8 - 4 - 2

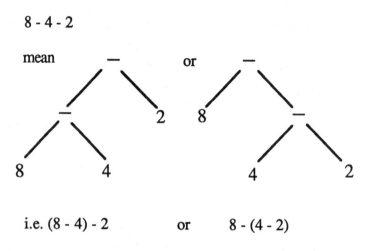

mean   or

i.e. (8 - 4) - 2   or   8 - (4 - 2)

This ambiguity would cause inconsistency, because of the unpredictable nature of the results. You can see that it would be a good idea to forbid such ambiguous declarations.

Forcing a precedence of zero

It is possible to force a structure to have a precedence of zero by enclosing it within parentheses. Everything within parentheses would be treated in the normal way, as a structure, with the standard operator precedences applying within the parentheses. for example, if we define 'plus' and 'minus' to be operators we could make the following operator declarations:

        op(20, xfy, plus).
        op(20, xfy, minus).

If we then type:

?- **reveal(3 plus 4 minus 2).**

we get:

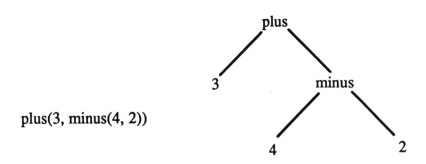

plus(3, minus(4, 2))

'plus' is the 'principal functor', i.e. the last operation to be performed, i.e. 3 + (4 - 2). If however we try:

reveal((3 plus 4) minus 2).

we get:

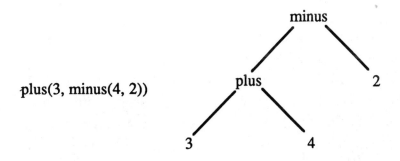

plus(3, minus(4, 2))

By bracketing the '3 plus 4' we give it a precedence of zero, tightening the binding of 'plus' to its arguments, and making 'minus' the principal functor. The lower the precedence the earlier the calculation.

Prefix and Postfix operators

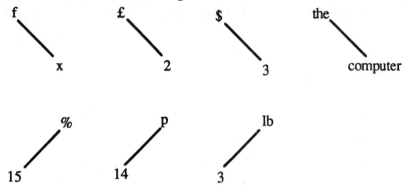

'f', '£', '$' and 'the' are prefix operators and '%', 'p' and 'lb' (Imperial pound - a unit of weight) is a postfix operator. A prefix operator appears before its argument. The same tenets for assigning precedence and associativity apply to prefix and postfix operators. For an example take:

the quick brown fox jumped over the lazy dog.

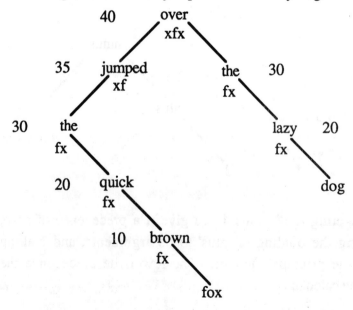

The declarations are:

```
op(40, xfx, over).
op(35, xf, jumped).
op(30, fx, the).
op(20, fx, lazy).
op(20, fx, quick).
op(10, fx, brown).
```

derived from the tree above.

Exercises

1. For the sentences below:

   a) draw the parse tree (sentential structure)
   b) assign the operator precedences
   c) assign operator associativity

the man eats the apple.
the man in the boat eats the red apple in the bowl.
the girl in the train eats the apple and the orange.

2. Make the necessary operator declarations to enable the predicate 'member' to be written in the following form:

```
X member_of [X | _].
X member_of [_ | Tail] :-
        X member_of Tail.
```

3. Make the necessary declarations to enable the predicate 'append' to be written in the following way:

[] appended_to List gives List.

[Item | List1] appended_to List2 gives [Item | List3] :-
  List1 append_to List2 gives List3.

CHAPTER 12

A Meta-level Expert System

We introduced operators in the last chapter in order to write a more superior version of an expert system. A meta program is a program which manipulates programs as data. In this chapter we write the rules for our expert system in a kind of natural language. As a result we also write our own interpreter to answer the queries. The interpreter is said to be a meta interpreter because the domain rules equate to a different notation for Prolog rules, therefore the interpreter takes a rule-based program and makes inferences using this knowledge.

We will develop an expert system for diagnosing why a car will not start. The rules are:

rule 1:   if   car wont start
            then   check engine.
rule 2:   if   car wont start
            then   check starter.
rule 3:   if   check engine   and
                      engine turns slowly
            then   boost starter.
rule 4:   if   check engine   and
                      engine turns slowly
            then   charge battery.
rule 5:   if   check engine   and
                      engine turns slowly
            then   push_start.
rule 6:   if   check engine   and

		engine turns normally	
	then	check ignition.	
rule 7:	if	check starter	and
		engine turns normally	
	then	check fuel.	
rule 8:	if	check starter	and
		starter whirrs	
	then	tap starter.	
rule 9:	if	check starter	and
		starter clicks	
	then	push_start.	
rule 10:	if	check starter	and
		starter stuck	
	then	engage gear	and
		release hand_brake	and
		rock car.	
rule 11:	if	check ignition	
	then	check connections.	
rule 12:	if	check ignition	
	then	check distributor.	
rule 13:	if	check ignition	
	then	check coil.	
rule 14:	if	check ignition	
	then	check plugs.	
rule 15:	if	check distributor	
	then	check distributor_cap	and
		check points.	
rule 16:	if	check points	
	then	check gap	and
		clean contacts.	
rule 17:	if	check ignition	
	then	check weather.	
rule 18:	if	check weather	and
		weather damp	

	then	clean leads	and
		dry leads.	
rule 19:	if	check plugs	
	then	clean plugs	and
		dry plugs.	
rule 20:	if	check fuel	
	then	check petrol.	
rule 21:	if	petrol_tank empty	
	then	fill petrol_tank.	
rule 22:	if	check fuel	and
		not petrol_tank empty	
	then	check fuel_leak.	

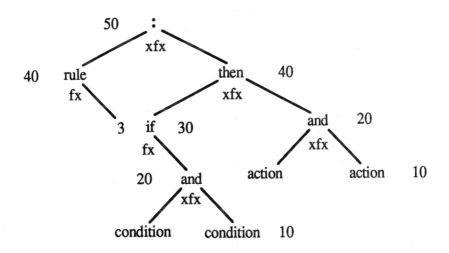

In order to allow the rules to be input in this format, we need to make the relevant operator declarations. First we need to draw the rule structure as shown above. From the diagram clearly we have to define the following operators:

```
?- op(50, xfx, :).
?- op(40, xfx, then).
```

```
?- op(40, fx, rule).
?- op(40, fx, fact).
?- op(30, fx, if).
?- op(20, xfx, and).
```

In addition we need to declare the following operators for the conditions and actions:

```
?- op(10, xfx  wont).
?- op(10, xfx, turns).
?- op(10, fx, check).
?- op(10, fx, charge).
?- op(10, fx, tap).
?- op(10, fx, boost).
?- op(10, fx, engage).
?- op(10, fx, release).
?- op(10, fx, rock).
?- op(10, fx, clean).
?- op(10, fx, dry).
?- op(10, fx, fill).
?- op(10, xf, whirrs).
?- op(10, xf, clicks).
?- op(10, xf, damp).
?- op(10, xf, stuck).
?- op(10, xf, empty).
```

The facts can be entered in the same way, e.g.

```
fact 1: car wont start.
fact 2: engine turns slowly.
```

The facts should be entered in such a way that they match the precondition of at least one rule. The structure of a fact is:

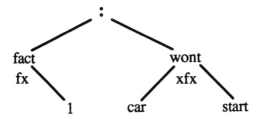

In addition to the declarations already made for the rules, all that is required for the facts is to declare 'fact' as prefix operator.

We can now start to implement our interpreter. We will implement a backward chaining interpreter, that is, we will make inferences and if they are correct the system will tell us why. The first thing to do is to enable a query of the facts. We will call the predicate 'backward'. To enable a query of the following type:

?- backward(engine turns slowly).

To which the system responds 'yes'; or the query:

?- backward(engine turns X).

to which the system responds:

X = slowly
more y/n

and for a final example when querying facts, if the fact is not there the query should fail. For example:

?- backward(engine turns normally).

returns the answer:

no.

The Prolog code for the first backward clause is:

> **backward(Fact) :-**
> **fact N: Fact.**

Our next task is to write a clause which when given a conjunction of facts to search for, succeeds if they are both present in the database. For example:

> **?- backward(car wont start and engine turns**
> **slowly).**

responds:

> yes.

or:

> **?- backward(car wont start and engine turns Y).**

responds:

> Y = slowly.

The clause looks like this:

> **backward(Fact1 and Fact2) :-**
> **backward(Fact1),**
> **backward(Fact2).**

We next require a clause which, if it does not find the fact in the database, looks at the conclusion part of the rules in turn and tries to prove their conditions. For example:

?- backward(charge battery).

Here there is no fact recommending the battery be recharged, so the interpreter scans the rules and finds that the conclusion part of rule 4 matches the query. That means we should charge the battery if the conditions of rule 4 are satisfied, namely: 'car wont start' and 'engine turns slowly'. As these facts are in the database the query succeeds. The third clause to backward is therefore:

backward(Action) :-
  rule N: if Condition then Action,
  backward(Condition).

There is one more clause that we require to make the interpreter complete. If for some reason the interpreter fails to find a relation as a fact and also fails to find the relation in the conclusion part of a rule, then it should be able to enquire of the user whether the relation is true. The user can reply "y" or "n". If the user responds "y" then the fact should be added to the list of facts already known to be true. The fact could be indexed as being told rather than being numbered. For example:

?- backward(fill petrol_tank).

produces the following response from the system:

is it true that petrol_tank empty ? [y/n]

to which the user can respond "y" to add the fact to the database, or "n" to look for another cause of the car not starting.

The actual implementation is not as difficult as it may seem:

```
backward(X) :-
  write(' is it true that '),
  write(X),
  write('  [y/n]     '),
  get("y"),
  assert(fact told: X).
```

The whole interpreter consists of the four clauses detailed above, and appears below for clarity:

```
backward(Fact) :-          /* backward chaining a fact */
  fact N: Fact.            /*  then look for that fact  */
backward(Fact1 and Fact2) :-    /* If a conjunction */
  backward(Fact1),        /* look for each conjunct */
  backward(Fact2).                /* separately */
backward(Action) :-    /* if matches rule action then */
  rule N: if Condition then Action, /* backward */
  backward(Condition).  /* chain rule's conditions */
backward(X) :-              /* if condition not found */
  write(' is it true that '),    /* then ask the user */
  write(X),
  write('  [y/n]     '),
  get("y"),                      /*  if it is true then */
  assert(fact told: X).    /* add it to the database */
```

The rules detailed at the start of the chapter could also be used in a forward chaining manner, to generate a list of things to check in order to overcome the problem of the car not starting. Forward chaining makes inferences based on the conditions of the rules that can be satisfied. The conditions can be satisfied either from the database or from a list of facts entered by the user.

This time the code will be presented first and then an explanation offered.

```
forward(List) :-
    rule X: if Condition then Action, /* find a rule */
    check(Condition, List),/* see if conditions match */
    not fact N: Action,      /* if the fact is not known */
    assert(fact inferred: Action), /* add to database */
    write(Action),        /* inform the user of the action */
    nl,                          /* write a newline */
    forward(Action),        /* see if anymore rules fire */
    fail.                   /* backtrack to try all rules */
forward(_).


check(A  and  B, List) :-   /* if conjunction of conds */
    check(A,  List),  /* check each conjunct separately */
    check(B,  List).
check(A,  List) :-    /* check a condition see to if it's a */
    member(A,  List);  /* member of user's fact list or */
    fact N: A.          /* if it is already in the database */


member(X,  X) :- !.
member(X,  [X |  _]) :- !.
member(X,  [__  | T]) :-
    member(X,  T).
```

The predicate works by taking the first rule and seeing if its conditions are satisfied. If the conditions are satisfied and the fact is not already known to the system (i.e. is not already in the database) then it is asserted into the database. If this check were not made then upon each recursive cycle through the predicate, the same rule would have its conditions matched and assert into the database, thereby causing an infinite loop, until the machine runs out of workspace. Once the fact has been asserted, and the user informed, the system recurses to try all the rules again to see if any of the earlier rules will now fire as a result of this new inferred piece of information.

To run the forward chaining expert system detailed above, type in the query:

?- forward([car wont start, engine turns
                                            normally]).

The system replies:

check engine
check starter
boost starter
charge battery
push_start
check ignition
check connections
check distributor
check coil
check plugs
check distributor_cap and check points
check points
check gap
clean contacts
check weather
clean plugs
dry plugs
check fuel
check petrol

This information is useful in a different way to that produced by backward chaining. The thing to remember though, is that the way in which the program is executed depends on you. Meta-level programming requires a little more work but results in much greater flexibility and expressiveness of the input and interface. It would not require too much time and effort to develop a more sophisticated backward chaining interpreter that allowed you to ask 'how' and 'why' questions, i.e. how a conclusion was reached, and why a question was asked of the user. This development is left as an exercise for you to do.

The interpreters are independent of the knowledge base. A second knowledge base is supplied below for you to play with. Remember you will need to make some operator declarations before the rules can be used.

rule 1: if X isa plant then X isa herb.
rule 2: if X isa tree then X isa plant.
rule 3: if X isa insect then X isa animal.
rule 4: if X isa mammal then X isa animal.
rule 5: if X isa fish then X isa animal.
rule 6: if X isa beetle then X isa insect.
rule 7: if X isa fish then cat eats X.
rule 8: if X isa fish and Y isa insect then X eats Y.
rule 9: if X isa bird and Y isa insect then X eats Y.
rule 10: if X eats Y then X likes Y.

fact 1: vole isa mammal.
fact 2: cat isa mammal.
fact 3: trout isa fish.
fact 4: perch isa fish.
fact 5: minnow isa fish.
fact 6: ladybird isa beetle.
fact 7: fox isa mammal.
fact 8: parsely isa herb.
fact 9: oak isa tree.

Summary

* we looked at meta level programming.
* we implemented a backward chaining interpreter.
* we looked at the implementation of a forward chaining
  interpreter.

Exercise

1. Extend the backward chaining program so that when it asks if
   something is true, if you respond with **why**, it prints out the
   rule that it is trying to satisfy.
2. Extend the program further by having it respond to successive
   whys by printing out all the rules that it is trying to prove at
   corresponding levels.

CHAPTER 13

How to Cross a River Without Getting Wet

The problem is that you are a farmer crossing a river on the way to market with a chicken, a bag of grain and a fox. If left unattended, the fox will eat the chicken and the chicken will eat the grain. Your boat will only hold you and one of the items across the river each time. Your task is to work out a sequence of crossings that will effect a safe transfer of you and all your belongings.

The initial state of the world can be represented as:

```
isat(man, left).
isat(chicken, left).
isat(fox, left).
isat(grain, left).
```

You may notice that we have not represented the boat explicitly as it would always be with the man who needs to row it. The river is represented by its two banks:

```
otherbank(left, right).
otherbank(right, left).
```

Crossing the river would mean deleting the assertion that the man is at a bank and asserting that he is on the other bank.

```
cross :-
    retract(isat(man, X)),
```

```
        otherbank(X,  Y),
        assert(isat(man,  Y)),
        demons.
```

Moving an object is similar to crossing but with the added complication that it also needs to be deleted at one bank and asserted on the other bank.

```
move(X)  :-
        retract(isat(X,  B)),
        retract(isat(man,  B)),
        otherbank(B,  C),
        assert(isat(X,  C)),
        assert(isat(man,  C)),
        demons.
```

We should avoid leaving the chicken alone with either the grain or the fox, otherwise when the man comes back from the other bank he will find only the chicken or the fox respectively.

```
demons :-
        isat(chicken,  X),
        isat(grain,  X),
        not(isat(man,  X)),
        write("The chicken has eating the grain"), nl,
        retract(isat(grain,  X)),
        demons.
demons :-
        isat(fox,  X),
        isat(chicken,  X),
        not(isat(man,  X)),
        write("The fox has eaten the chicken."), nl,
        retract(isat(chicken,  X)).
demons.
```

Searching for a solution

Doing complex things in the world is a matter of stringing together constituent actions in the CORRECT ORDER. At this time we shall consider the situations in which finding the correct order is rather clearly problematical - the domain of puzzle solving.

In order to understand the SOLUTION sequence you need to know that there is a goal of getting things to the other side, without anything being eaten, and further that the 'laws' of the world make it impossible to achieve this goal if the chicken is left with either the fox or the grain.

So starting from the initial state of the world with everything at the Left Bank we can see that we have four choices each of which leads us to a new world state: in three of these something will get eaten. We can think about the puzzle-solving activity as applying the available moves to the initial state, then to its daughter state then to theirs and so on - exploring a tree of possibilities (see Figure 13.1).

It can be seen from the search tree that two solutions exist:

move(chicken)	move(chicken)
move(man)	move(man)
move(fox)	move(grain)
move(chicken)	move(chicken)
move(grain)	move(fox)
move(man)	move(man)
move(chicken)	move(chicken)

The solutions represent a series of moves from one state to another from the START STATE to the GOAL STATE. The basic idea of these 'daughter' states can be captured by a function 'search' that calls a subordinate - 'trymoves' - which calls itself. Each new call of 'trymoves' is a new daughter state.

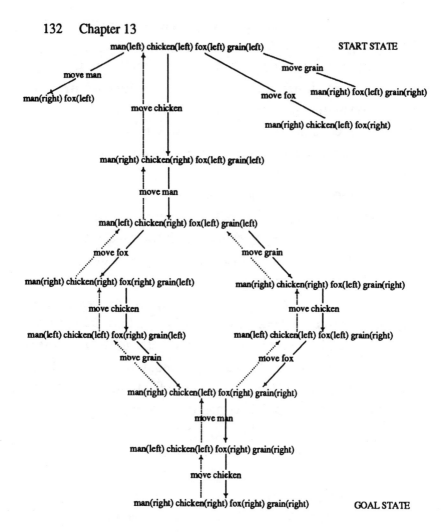

Fig. 13.1 Tree of possible moves

This second package solves the puzzle automatically. There are other more sophisticated solutions one of which is detailed at the end of the chapter. The solution can be changed to deal with other puzzles in the 'Missionaries and cannibals' class of puzzles.

opposite(left, right).
opposite(right, left).

```
cross :-
    ndretract(isat(man,  X)),
    opposite(X,  Y),
    ndassert(isat(man,  Y)).


move(man) :-  fail.
move(X)  :-
    ndretract(isat(X,  B)),
    ndretract(isat(man,  B)),
    opposite(B,  C),
    ndassert(isat(X,  C)),
    ndassert(isat(man,  C)).
```

The following two lines are non-deterministic assert and retract.
On backtracking, these will undo their side-effects.

```
ndassert(X)  :-  asserta(X).
ndassert(X)  :-  retract(X), !, fail.


ndretract(X)  :-  X, doretract(X).


doretract(X)  :-  retract(X).
doretract(X)  :-  asserta(X), !, fail.


retractall(X)  :-  retract(X), retractall(X).
retractall(_).
```

A move is no good if the chicken and either the fox or
the grain is on one bank and the man is on the opposite bank

```
nogood :-
    isat(grain,  X),
    isat(chicken,  X),
    opposite(X,  Y),
```

```
        isat(man,  Y).
nogood  :-
        isat(fox,  X),
        isat(chicken,  X),
        opposite(X,  Y),
        isat(man,  Y).
```

It is safe for the man to cross on his own if the resulting state is good, in other words not nogood.

```
safecross  :-
        cross,
        not(nogood)
        notestate,
        ndassert(done(cross)).
```

It is safe to move something to the opposite bank if the resulting state is not nogood.

```
safemove(X)  :-
        move(X),
        not(nogood),
        notestate,
        ndassert(done(move(X))).
```

Find out where everything is and make a note, so that this state (if not already tried) is not tried later during the solution.

```
notestate :-
        getlist(L,  isat(X,  Y)),
        donote(L).
```

Make a note in the database to say that we have been to this state.

```
donote(L) :-
    permute(L, K),
    been(K),
    !,
    fail.
donote(L) :- ndassert(been(L)).
```

There are various ways of achieving some **Thing** at some **Bank**. These differing ways are implemented as things to try.

```
try(Thing, Bank) :- isat(Thing, Bank), !.
try(man, Bank) :- safecross.
try(Thing, Bank) :-
    isat(man, Bank),
    safecross,
    safemove(thing).
try(Thing, Bank) :-
    isat(man, Bank),
    isat(X, Bank),
    safemove(X),
    safemove(Thing).
try(Thing, Bank) :- safemove(Thing).
```

The problem is solved when everything is safely on the right bank.

```
solved :-
    isat(man, right),
    isat(fox, right),
    isat(chicken, right),
    isat(grain, right).
```

Achieve a set of goals to try.

```
achmany([]).
achmany([A|B]) :-
    membership(X,  Y,  [A|B]),
    achlist(X,  Y).


achlist(X,  Y) :-  X,  achmany(Y),  !.
```

To solve the problem try and achieve each of the objects on the right-hand side.

```
solve :-
    start,
    achmany([try(fox,  right),  try(chicken,  right),
    try(grain,  right),  try(man,  right)]),
    solved.

solution :-
    listing(isat),
    listing(done).
```

Generate all permutations of a list.

```
permute([],  []).
permute(X,  [A|C]) :-
    membership(A,  B,  X),
    permute(B,  C).
```

Generate all members of a list for producing permutations of a list.

/* membership(An item, Rest of the list, List) */

```
membership(X, Y, [X|Y]).
membership(X, [Y|P], [Y|Z]) :-
    membership(X, P, Z).
```

/* Note taking functions */

```
getlist(L, X) :-
    asserta(constructing([])),
    X ,
    retract(constructing(T)),
    asserta(constructing([X|T])),
    fail.
getlist(L, X) :- retract(constructing(L)).
```

```
start:-
    retractall(done(K)),
    retractall(been(L)),
    assert(isat(man,  left)),
    assert(isat(chicken,  left)),
    assert(isat(fox,  left)),
    assert(isat(grain,  left)),
    notestate.
```

To solve the problem, enter the query:

```
?- solve.
```

the 'start' goal simply initialises the database to the four 'isat' facts. Any assertions from a previous run will be removed so that they do not affect the solution. 'achmany' then tries to achieve the man, the chicken, the fox and the grain on the right bank. In order to achieve one goal another goal may be undone, so after the first 'pass' when the goal 'solved' is asked the state of the problem is:

isat(man, right).
isat(chicken, left).
isat(fox, right).
isat(grain, right).

'solved' therefore fails and causes backtracking to 'achmany', which tries to achieve the four goals again. This time all that is required is for the man to return and pick up his chicken.

Although automatic in its execution this is a badly written Prolog program for the following reasons:

✍ Managing the database requires extra predicates for nondeterministic assertion to and retraction from the database.

✍ The uncertain order of the 'isat' clauses, we need to find all the permutations of a state to ensure that we have not already tried it.

✍ Obtaining permutations requires a bit of clever Prolog programming and is far from intuitive.

✍ As a consequence of clumsy construction, understanding and debugging the program is made difficult.

✍ We have deliberately used terse variable names to make understanding that little bit more difficult.

✍ The program lacks structure.

The program illustrates how to approach problem solving utilising the database. It is much better however, to use Prolog's base data structure, the list, to represent the state of things rather than the Prolog database. Below is detailed the same automatic solution to the man getting his possessions across the river. At first glance this program looks more complex it is in fact simpler, and a better approach to the problem for the following reasons:

- There are no unnecessary list handling routines to write.
- The execution is more transparent
- Recursion is more efficient than backtracking
- The program is more readable

The first thing we want to do is to decide upon a representation for the start and goal states. The representation must capture the features of the problem, and yet, not be too complicated. The simplest representation is:

```
start_state([fox(right),chicken(right),
        grain(right),man(right)]).
goal_state([fox(left),  chicken(left),  grain(left),
        man(left)]).
```

In order to get the start state all we need to do is type the query:

```
?- start_state(Start).
```

We also need to define the left and right banks as being opposite to each other, so that when we move from one bank to the other we move either from the left bank to the right bank or vice-versa.

```
otherbank(right, left).
otherbank(left, right).
```

The next task is to define a move generator, which produces all the moves that could be made from a given state. No test is made as to the legality of the move, all we want is to move. We can write a separate test to see if the move is illegal. The four possible moves are:

1. move the man
2. move the fox and the man
3. move the chicken and the man
4. move the grain and the man

We must declare the operator in order to have our moves written in the form:

move(Object to Destination, State).

?- op(20, xfx, to).

```
move([fox(A), chicken(B), grain(C), man(Bank)],
        [fox(A), chicken(B), grain(C), man(Opposite)],
        move(man to Opposite,
        [fox(A),chicken(B),grain(C),man(Opposite)])) :-
    otherbank(Bank, Opposite).
move([fox(Bank), chicken(B), grain(C), man(Bank)],
        [fox(Opposite),chicken(B),grain(C),man(Opposite)],
        move(fox to Opposite, NewState)) :-
    otherbank(Bank, Opposite).
move([fox(A), chicken(Bank), grain(C), man(Bank)],
        [fox(A), chicken(Opposite), grain(C), man(Opposite)],
        move(chicken to Opposite, NewState)) :-
    otherbank(Bank, Opposite).
move([fox(A), chicken(B), grain(Bank), man(Bank)],
        [fox(A), chicken(B), grain(Opposite), man(Opposite)],
        move(grain to Opposite, NewState)) :-
    otherbank(Bank, Opposite).
```

The move generator takes three arguments, a problem state, the state after the move, and a record of the move. The record of the move takes the form of a short statement, e.g. fox to left, with the state that has been moved to. You may have noticed that the first move has a longer third line than the rest. The reason for this, is that the moves make a note of the state that is being moved to, in order to prevent cyclic moves. The first move details all the information in the clause just as an example, but since the new state is the same as the second argument then all we need to do is specify a variable NewState and force the instantiation in the calling routine (see the predicate cross later), rather like the way that the first line of append works:

?- **append([], [a,b,c], List).**

matches:

append([], L, L).

forcing List to take on the same value as L, which has taken the value [a,b,c], therefore List (in the query) is [a,b,c].

After specifying the legal move generator, we ought to check that the move is legal (not illegal), there are only two illegal situations to be avoided. The first is if the fox and the chicken are on one bank and the man is on the other bank. The second is if the chicken and the grain are on the one bank and the man is on the opposite bank. These situations can be represented thus:

illegal([fox(Bank), chicken(Bank), grain(_),
                                man(Opp)]) :-
        otherbank(Bank, Opp).
illegal([fox(_), chicken(Bank), grain(Bank),
                                man(Opp)]) :-
        otherbank(Bank, Opp).

To call the move generator we need a higher level goal that

obtains moves and then tests to see if the move is legal.

```
cross(Goal, Plan, Plan, Goal) :- !.
cross(State, Sofar, Plan, Goal):-
    move(State, Newstate, move(X, Newstate)),
    not illegal(Newstate),
    not tried(Newstate),
    assert(tried(Newstate)),
    cross(Newstate, [move(X, Newstate) | Sofar],
                                    Plan,Goal).
```

Notice how the binding of the variable Newstate in the structure
move(X, Newstate) is done by the Prolog interpreter.

```
toplevel :-
    retractall(tried(_)),
    start_state(Start),
    goal_state(Goal),
    cross(Start,[],Plan,Goal),
    show_plan(Plan).

show_plan([]):-!.
show_plan([move(X,H)|T]):-
    show_plan(T), nl,
      write(X).
```

CHAPTER 14
Searching

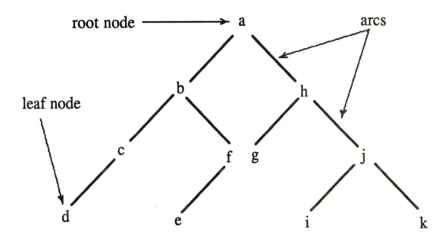

Fig. 14.1 Tree structure illustrated diagrammatically

Trees are a useful data structure which can be used to store data in a structured manner. By structured we do not necessarily mean in an ordered manner. Of course the size of the tree can become immense. In order to retrieve information the tree needs to be searched.

There are many search algorithms that exist. We will look at the following:

> depth first search

> breadth first search

> Best first search (A^T Algorithm)

> Heuristic guided best first search (A^* algorithm)

Definitions

State space   the space of all allowed problem or game states.

Nodes   represent individual problem states

Arcs   connect states via a single move/operation

Operators   a means of traversing the tree, i.e. making moves

Start Node   the initial problem state

Goal state   the desired solution state. There may be more than one solution

A solution   a path from start node to goal node.

A tree   a state space where it is not possible to return to a previously visited state.

A graph   a state space where it is possible to return to a previously visited state.

Evaluation criteria

The following terms are used to assess search algorithms

optimal -   path from start to goal with the least accumulated cost, or for equal (or no) cost, the shortest path.

admissable -   expends the least amount of effort in returning the optimal solution. The only nodes visited are those along the solution path.

Whenever data is stored in a tree like fashion, typically game playing and problem solving then search algorithms can be used to simplify the solution of a problem, or improve our chances of winning. Sometimes it may be sufficient to find any solution, sometimes we want only the 'best' solution. The best solution may simply be the shortest path (if the cost associated with each arc is the same), or if the cost associated with the arcs varies then this will be the path with the lowest incurred cost.

If the number of successors per node is the branching factor, there is no reason why the branching factor cannot vary throughout the tree, our only requirement is that we have access to the successors of each node.

Graphs

Whenever it is possible to return to a previous node then the tree is referred to as a graph (Figure 14.2), but this may still be drawn as a tree (Figure 14.3).

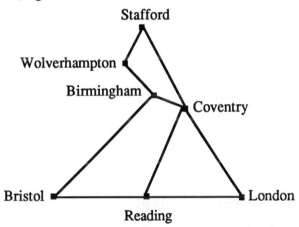

Fig. 14.2 A portion of the British Rail network (a graph)

It is possible to go between stations travelling in either direction.

Combinatorial explosion

In all except trivial cases a full search is untenable. A full exploration of state space would involve exploring each possible path until either:

☞   it reaches a goal

☞   it reaches a state from which the goal cannot be attained

☞   it reaches a state with no new successors (i.e. that have not been visited via some other route).

☞   the path is known to be worse than some other path.

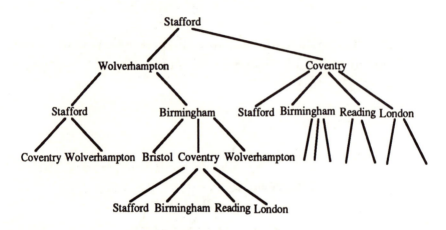

Fig. 14.3 Tree representation of the graph

Complexity of the problem

The branching factor is the number of successors that exist for any node (see Figure 14.4). The branching factor has been limited to three for simplicity, but could be any size. In chess game playing, the tree of possible moves can have branching factors of hundreds at some stages of the game. In the domain of chess the size of the tree is b^n, where b is the average number of moves per board position (approximately 35); n is the average depth at which checkmate is achieved, at a high standard this is in excess of one hundred. The number of nodes is therefore

$$35^{100} \approx 2.5 \times 10^{154}$$

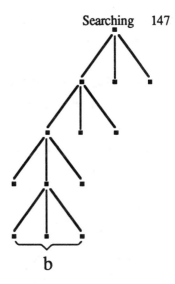

If b is uniform

No. of nodes at depth

N is b^n

Fig. 14.4 Branching factor

If we are able to examine a node every nanosecond (10^{-9} seconds), then we need centuries to explore the whole tree!

Programming a state space search

We require:

- A way of representing the states
- A way of representing the operators and hence programming the legal move generator
- A way of specifying a start and goal state and a way of recognising a goal state
- A search strategy

Depth first searching

A depth first search is a traversal of the tree in a left first depth first manner, going as far left and as deep as possible looking for the required node. Each non terminal node has successors which we need to look at.

We will make use of a data structure called a list of *open* nodes. These are the nodes whose predecessors have been examined. The way in which nodes are put onto our list of open nodes determines the search strategy.

Depth first algorithm

1. Place the start node in a list called OPEN.
2. If OPEN is empty then there is no way of getting from the start node to the goal node.
3. Take the first node from the OPEN list, if this is the goal node then success.
4. If not then generate a list of all the nodes that can be reached from the node removed from the open list (i.e. the node's direct successors) and add this list to the front of the OPEN list. Add the node to another list called CLOSED (the list of nodes that have been visited).
5. Repeat from 2.

The order in which nodes are visited during a breadth first search is a, b, c, d, e, f, g, h, i, j, k. OPEN goes through the following transitions

OPEN	visit	CLOSED
[a]	a	[]
[b, g]	b	[a]
[c, e, g]	c	[b, a]
[d, e, g]	d	[c, b, a]
[e, g]	e	[d, c, b, a]
[f, g]	f	[e, d, c, b, a]
[g]	g	[f, e, d, c, b, a]
[h, i]	h	[g, f, e, d, c, b, a]
[i]	i	[h, g, f, e, d, c, b, a]

[j, k]	j	[i, h, g f, e, d, c, b, a]
[k]	k	[j, i, h, g, f, e, d, c, b, a]
[]		

During a depth first search in order to prevent cyclic traversals we make the following modification to the algorithm. If a node is already on CLOSED then do not generate a list of its successors as they will already have been put onto OPEN (when the node was first closed).

Exercise

Write a program to do a depth first search of the following road network. Use a structure OPEN which is a list of nodes to be visited, a second structure CLOSED can be used to keep a record of the nodes that have already been visited.

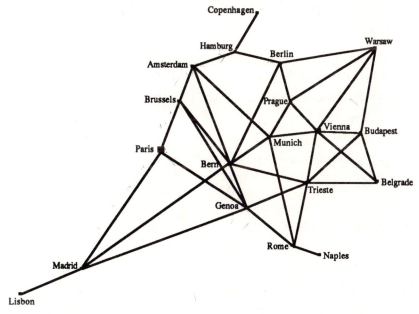

Fig. 14.5 Major European cities

The paths between the cities in Figure 14.5 may be represented by the following Prolog facts.

path(amsterdam, brussels).   path(amsterdam, bern).
path(amsterdam, munich).   path(amsterdam, hamburg).
path(belgrade, budapest).   path(belgrade, trieste).
path(belgrade, vienna).   path(berlin, hamburg).
path(berlin, warsaw).   path(berlin, bern).
path(berlin, prague).   path(bern, trieste).
path(bern, madrid).   path(bern, brussels).
path(bern, genoa).   path(bern, munich).
path(brussels, genoa).   path(brussels, paris).
path(budapest, warsaw).   path(budapest, vienna).
path(budapest, trieste).   path(copenhagen, hamburg).
path(genoa, paris).   path(genoa, rome).
path(genoa, madrid).   path(genoa, trieste).
path(lisbon, madrid).   path(madrid, paris).
path(munich, prague).   path(munich, rome).
path(munich, vienna).   path(naples, rome).
path(prague, vienna).   path(prague, warsaw).
path(rome, trieste).   path(trieste, vienna).
path(vienna, warsaw).

The top level of the predicate is simply expressed, being based upon the algorithm.

```
search(Start, Goal) :-
        depth_first([Start], [], Goal).

depth_first([], _, _) :- !, fail.
depth_first([Goal | _], _, Goal) :- !.
depth_first([Node | T], Closed, Goal) :-
            not member(Node, Closed),
            get_successors(Node, Succs),
```

```
            append(Succs, T, Open),
            depth_first(Open, [Node I Closed], Goal).
depth_first([_ I Open], Closed, Goal) :-
            depth_first(Open, Closed, Goal).
```

The first clause of depth_first is optional, and is supplied here for completeness, as the algorithm says, if OPEN is empty then the search has failed. There is however, no need to include the clause as the failure of the clause is implicit whenever OPEN is empty. None of the three clauses would match an empty first argument, therefore the call would fail.

```
get_successors(Node, Succs):-
            findall(X, (path(Node, X); path(X, Node)), Succs).
```

findall is a very useful utility for collecting all the items that satisfy a goal. Here findall is used to return a list Succs, which contains all of the unique items that satisfy the goal

```
            path(Node, X); path(X, Node)
```

that is, all of the nodes X, that we are able to get to from Node. The implementation of findall is shown below. It is worth keeping a copy of it along with the other useful predicates that are not built in predicates (member, append, etc.).

```
findall(Item, Goal, _) :-
            asserta(found(terminator)),
            call(Goal),
            not found(Item),
            asserta(found(Item)),
            fail.
findall(_, _, List) :-
            collect([], List).
```

```
collect(Sofar, List) :-
        retract(found(Item)),
        Item = terminator,
        collect([Item | Sofar], List).
collect(L, L).


append([], L, L).
append([H | T], List2, [H | List3]) :-
        append(T, List2, List3).


member(Item, [Item | _]).
member(Item, [_ | Tail]) :- member(Item, Tail).
```

This solution is fine except that if we enter:

```
        search(paris, london).
```

It spends a lot of time going round in circles. We need to prune the list of successors by testing to see if any of the successors are already on OPEN, or if they have already been visited.

```
depth_first([Goal | _], _, Goal) :- !.
depth_first([Node | T], Closed, Goal) :-
        not member(Node, Closed),
        get_successors(Node, Succs),
        prune(Succs, T, Closed, New_succs),
        append(New_succs, T, Open),
        !,
        depth_first(Open, [Node | Closed], Goal).
depth_first([_ | Open], Closed, Goal) :-
        depth_first(Open, Closed, Goal).
```

```
prune(Succs, Open, Closed, New_succs) :-
      check(Succs, Open, Succs2),
      check(Succs2, Closed, New_succs).


check([], L, []) :-!.
check([H | T], List, New_succs) :-
      member(H, List),
      check(T, List, New_succs).
check([H | T], List, [H | New_succs]) :-
      check(T, List, New_succs).
```

Returning the path

The path traversed may be retrieved by putting the predecessor of
a node in with the node so that OPEN consists of a list of pairs

[[node1, predecessor1], [node2, predecessor2]]

Consider the original example:

OPEN	visit	CLOSED Node Pointer
[[a, []]]	a	[]
[[b, a], [g, a]]	b	[[a,[]]]
[[c, b], [e, b], [g, a]]	c	[[b,a],[a, []]]
[[d, c], [e, b], [g, a]]	d	[[c,b],[b, a],[a, []]]
[[e, b], [g, a]]	e	[[d,c],[c, b],[b, a],[a, []]]
[[f, e], [g, a]]	f	[[e,b],[d, c],[c, b],[b, a],[a, []]]
[[g, a]]	g	[[f,e],[e, b],[d, c],[c, b],[b, a],[a,[]]]
. . .	.	. . .

The path may be constructed by looking at the nodes on closed.

Beginning with the Goal node

1.   Take a node, print it out.
2.   Make the predecessor the current node.
3.   If the current node is the Start node then halt.
4.   Otherwise take the next pair in CLOSED, if the node is
      the same as current node then repeat from 1.
5.   If the node is not the same repeat from 4.

The call is of the form:

        ?- print_path(Closed, Goal, Start).

The predicate is

```
print_path([ [Start | _] | _], _, Start) :-
        write('the path is from '),
        write(Start).
print_path([ [Node, Pred | _] | T], Node, Start) :-
        print_path(T, Pred, Start),
        write('to'),
        write(Node),
        nl.
print_path([ _ | T], Node, Start) :-
        print_path(T, Node, Start).
```

This is a clever implementation which exploits the ordering of
OPEN (which is in reverse order). The predicate recurses down
to the Start node printing the rest of the text as the recursion
unwinds.
        Test the printing of the path by entering the query

        ?- depth_search(paris, vienna).

Summary of the depth first search

Blind search.

not optimal - expends a lot of unnecessary effort.

not admissable - will not find the best solution unless
there is only one solution.

Breadth first searching

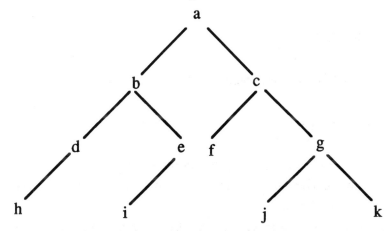

Simple tree illustrating a breadth first search

A breadth first search of this tree will visit the nodes in the
following order: a, b, c, d, e, f, g, h, i, j, k.

OPEN	visit	CLOSED
[a]	a	[]
[b, c]	b	[a]
[c, d, e]	c	[b, a]
[d, e, f, g]	d	[c, b, a]
[e, f, g, h]	e	[d, c, b, a]
[f, g, h, i]	f	[e, d, c, b, a]
[g, h, i]	g	[f, e, d, c, b, a]
[h, i, j, k]	h	[g, f, e, d, c, b, a]

[i, j, k]	i	[h, g, f, e, d, c, b, a]
[j, k]	j	[i, h, g f, e, d, c, b, a]
[k]	k	[j, i, h, g, f, e, d, c, b, a]
[]		

Breadth first algorithm

1. Place the start node in a list OPEN.
2. If OPEN is empty then a solution from the start to the goal node is unobtainable.
3. Take the first node from the list of OPEN nodes, if this is the goal node then succeed.
4. Otherwise:
    i)   Generate a list of the successors of the node removed from OPEN, and
    ii) add this list to the end of the OPEN list.
    iii) Add the node to another list called CLOSED (the list of nodes that have been visited).
    iv) If a node is already on CLOSED then do not generate a list of its successors as they will already have been put onto OPEN (when the node was first closed).
5. Repeat from step 2.

The implementation is the same as that of the depth first solution except that the top level is changed so that the list of successors is appended to the **end** of OPEN.

```
breadth_search(Start, Goal) :-
      breadth_first([Start], [], Goal).

breadth_first([Goal | _], _, Goal) :- !.
breadth_first([Node | T], Closed, Goal) :-
        not member(Node, Closed),
        get_successors(Node, Succs),
```

```
        prune(Succs, T, Closed, New_succs),
        append(T, New_succs, Open),
        !,
        breadth_first(Open, [Node I Closed], Goal).
breadth_first([_ I Open], Closed, Goal) :-
        breadth_first(Open, Closed, Goal).
```

Try the following query for a comparison of depth first and breadth first search:

?- breadth_search(paris, vienna).

The choice between a depth first and a breadth first strategy depends upon the way in which the solutions are stored.

If there are many solutions embedded deep within the tree and the branching factor is low, then a depth first search may be the most efficient. If however, the branching factor is high or solutions are obtainable at a shallow depth then a breadth first search is more likey to be the most efficient.

Both techniques however are blind and there is no knowledge to guide the search towards the solution(s). The A^T and A* (A star) algorithms make use of additional knowledge to guide the search.

Best first algorithm (A^T algorithm)

In the depth first and breadth first solutions we were not concerned with the amount of effort expended in producing a solution. Some applications require the shortest route between two nodes as opposed to any route. The best first algorithm deals with non-uniform costs. State space is a graph, i.e. there is more than one way to get to a node. The best first algorithm is the one that is guaranteed to return the best path between the start and goal nodes if one exists.

In order to determine the 'best' route their needs to be some criterion for determining the 'best' solution. We will consider the European cities of Figure 14.5 and the approximate road distances between the cities (Figure 14.6).

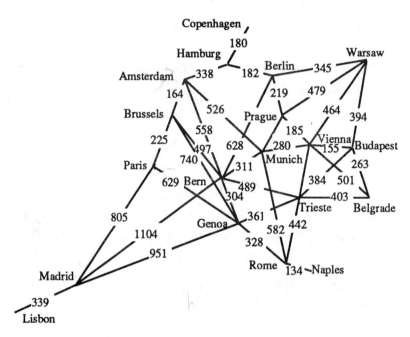

Fig. 14.6 European cities with road distances

The paths between the cities is extended to include the road distances between the cities as shown below.

path(amsterdam,brussels,164). path(amsterdam, bern, 558).
path(amsterdam, munich, 526). path(amsterdam, hamburg, 338).
path(belgrade, budapest, 263). path(belgrade, trieste, 403).
path(belgrade, vienna, 501).   path(berlin, hamburg, 182).
path(berlin, warsaw, 345).   path(berlin, bern, 628).
path(berlin, prague, 219).   path(bern, trieste, 489).
path(bern, madrid, 1104).   path(bern, brussels, 497).
path(bern, genoa, 304).   path(bern, munich, 311).

path(brussels, genoa, 740).   path(brussels, paris, 225).
path(budapest, warsaw, 394).   path(budapest, vienna, 155).
path(budapest, trieste, 384).   path(copenhagen, hamburg,180).
path(genoa, paris, 629).   path(genoa, rome, 328).
path(genoa, madrid, 951).   path(genoa, trieste, 361).
path(lisbon, madrid, 339).   path(madrid, paris, 805).
path(munich, prague, 174).   path(munich, rome, 582).
path(munich, vienna, 280).   path(naples, rome, 134).
path(prague, vienna, 185).   path(prague, warsaw, 479).
path(rome, trieste, 442).   path(trieste, vienna, 317).
path(vienna, warsaw, 464).

The best path will now be the shortest path. The distances can be assumed to be the 'cost' of getting from one node to another. The A^T algorithm is guaranteed to return the path with the lowest incurred cost.

The steps of the algorithm are:

1. Put the start node in a list OPEN.
2. If OPEN is empty then a solution from start to goal cannot be found.
3. Select the first node from OPEN, if this is the required node then succeed.
4. Otherwise, for each successor of the node
    5. Calculate the cost of reaching the successor from the node and add the cost of reaching N from the start node.
    6. Insert each node into OPEN so that the first item on OPEN is the one with the lowest cost from start that has not been explored. The last item in the list is the one with the maximum cost from start node that has not been explored.
    7. If two nodes have the same cost then the last one added to OPEN should be inserted after the one(s) of equal cost

that are already on OPEN.

8. If a node is already on OPEN then we need only make a note of the shortest route, changing the predecessor value if the new method of reaching the node is lower than the previous method.

9. Repeat from 2.

If the cost associated with each path is equal then the A^T algorithm performs the same as the breadth first algorithm.

Prolog implementation of best first search

The implementation in Prolog, will utilise OPEN and CLOSED again except that this time they are triples comprising:

- the node

- the predecessor of the node

- the cost of reaching the node from the start

If a successor node is found to be on OPEN, then the cost of reaching the node via this 'new' route is compared with the cost already found if this new route is shorter then the existing triple for that node is deleted and the new triple added to OPEN in ascending order of accumulated cost. The node at the head of the OPEN list will always be that with the shortest untried route so far.

```
at_search(Start, Goal) :-
        best_first(Goal, [ [Start, [], 0] ], [], Closed),
        print_path(Closed, Goal, Start).
```

```prolog
print_path([ [Start| _] | _], _, Start) :- !,
        write('the path is from '),
        write(Start), nl.
print_path([ [Node, Pred|_] | T], Node, Start) :-
        !,
        print_path(T, Pred, Start),
        write(' to '),
        write(Node),
        nl.
print_path([ _ | T], Node, Start) :-
        print_path(T, Node, Start).


best_first(Goal, [], _, _) :-
        write(' All nodes visited '),
        write(Goal),
        write(' not found.'),
        nl.
best_first(G, [[G, P, Cost] | T], C, [[G, P, Cost] | C]):-!.
best_first(G, [[N, P, C] | T], Closed, Visited):-
        not visited(N, Closed),
        get_succs([N, P, C], T, Open,[[N, P, C]|Closed]),
        !,
        best_first(G, Open, [[N, P, C] | Closed], Visited).
best_first(G, [Triple | T], Closed, Visited) :-
        best_first(G, T, Closed, Visited).
```

In essence the structure of the solution is the same as the solutions for depth first and breadth first searches, the difference is in the way that the successors are pruned (from the CLOSED list) then they are checked to see if they are already on OPEN before being added to OPEN.

```prolog
get_succs([Node, _, Cost], Open, Open2, Visited) :-
        findall(X, (path(X, Node, _); path(Node, X, _) ), L),
```

        prune(L, Visited, Unvisited),
        check_open(Node,Cost,Unvisited,Open,Open2).

The process of pruning the successors is to simply remove those
that are on CLOSED, i.e. have already been visited, and those
that are on OPEN.

prune([], _,[]).
prune([H | T], Closed, [H | Succs]):-
        not visited(H, Closed),
        prune(T, Closed, Succs).
prune([H | T], Closed, Succs) :-
        prune(T, Closed, Succs).

visited(Node, [[Node | _] | _]).
visited(Node, [_ | T]) :-
        visited(Node, T).

Checking if a node is already on OPEN requires, for each of the
unvisited successors, that if the node is already on OPEN then
we check that the shortest path to the node is the one that is
preserved on OPEN. If the node is not already on OPEN then
we simply add it to OPEN maintaining an ordering of ascending
order of accumulated costs to node.

check_open(_, _, [], Open, Open) :- !.
check_open(Node, Cost_to_n, [H | T], O, OPEN) :-
        opened(H, O),
        !,
        (path(Node, H, Cost_to_h); path(H, Node, Cost_to_h)),
        Total is Cost_to_n + Cost_to_h,
        shortest(H, Node, Total, O, Open2),
        check_open(Node, Cost_to_n, T, Open2, OPEN).
check_open(Node, Cost_to_n, [H | T], O, OPEN) :-

```
         (path(Node, H, Cost_to_h); path(H, Node, Cost_to_h)),
         Total is Cost_to_n + Cost_to_h,
         add_to_open(H, Node, Total, O, Open2),
         check_open(Node, Cost_to_n, T, Open2, OPEN).


opened(Node, [[Node | _] |_]) :- !.
opened(Node, [_ | T]) :-
         opened(Node, T).


shortest(N, Pred1,Cn, [[N, P, C] |T], [[N, P, C] |T]) :-
         C =< Cn.
shortest(N,Pred,Cn, [[N, P, C]|T], [[N, Pred, Cn]|T]) :-
         Cn < C.
shortest(Node, Pred, Cost, [H | T], [H | Z]) :-
         shortest(Node, Pred, Cost, T, Z).


add_to_open(N, P, Cn, [], [[N, P, Cn]]).
add_to_open(N,P,Cn,[[N1,P1,C]|T],[[N,P,Cn],[N1,P1,C]|T]):-
         Cn < C.
add_to_open(Node, Pred, Cost, [H | T], [H | Z]) :-
         add_to_open(Node, Pred, Cost, T,  Z).
```

Try the query

```
         ?- at_search(paris, vienna).
```


Summary of best first algorithm

- Guaranteed to find a solution
- Admissible, because the node selected from OPEN is
  guaranteed to be that with the minimum untried cost so
  far.

- Efficiency-optimality, the search has no sense of direction, and is still blind. It therefore wastes a lot of effort.

Knowledge guided best first (A* algorithm)

The best first search needs some guidance in order to make it optimal. This extra knowledge (heuristics) is supplied in the form of estimates of the remaining cost from a node to a goal. In our European road map traversal problem (Figure 14.6), the estimates are the airline distances from a node to the goal.

estimate(paris, vienna, 760).
estimate(brussels, vienna, 672).
estimate(madrid, vienna, 1332).
estimate(genoa, vienna, 522).
estimate(amsterdam, vienna, 690).
estimate(bern, vienna, 490).
estimate(munich, vienna, 264).
estimate(hamburg, vienna, 553).
estimate(trieste, vienna, 206).
estimate(rome, vienna, 570).
estimate(berlin, vienna, 386).
estimate(prague, vienna, 186).
estimate(vienna, vienna, 0).

A* selects the node of OPEN with the minimum estimate of total cost, where

estimate of total cost f(n) is the known cost (gn)
plus the estimate of getting from the node to the goal h(n).

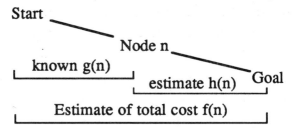

The steps of the algorithm are:

1. Put the start node in a list OPEN.
2. If OPEN is empty then a solution from start to goal cannot be found.
3. Select the first node from OPEN if this is the required node then succeed.
4. Otherwise, for each successor of the node
    5. Calculate the cost of reaching the successor from the node and add the cost of reaching N from the start node, this gives g(n). Add the estimated cost from the node to the goal to give f(n).
    6. Insert each node into OPEN so that the first item on OPEN is the one with the lowest estimated cost to the goal node that has not been explored. The last item in the list is the one with the maximum cost from start node that has not been explored.
    7. If two nodes have the same estimated cost then the last one added to OPEN should be inserted after the one(s) of equal cost that are already on OPEN.
8. Repeat from 2.

OPEN is now a list containing 4 items

   - the node

   - the nodes predecessor

- the cost of reaching the node from the Start node

- The estimated cost to the Goal from the node.

CLOSED consists of triples comprising

- the node

- the nodes predecessor

- the actual cost of reaching the node from the Start node

The Prolog code is provided below:

```
/************************************************
*                                              *
*     Name:  astar                             *
*                                              *
*     Description: initialises OPEN to the Start node     *
*                  initialises CLOSED to the empty list   *
*                  calls the A* algorithm and displays the result. *
*                                              *
*     Inputs: [arg1] the Start node            *
*             [arg2] the Goal node             *
*                                              *
*     Output: [arg3] the list of nodes on CLOSED  *
*                                              *
************************************************/

astar(Start, Goal, Closed) :-
      (estimate(Start, Goal, Fn); estimate(Goal, Start, Fn)),
      !,
```

```
        explore(Goal, [ [Start, [], 0, Fn] ], [], Closed),
        follow(Start, Goal, Closed).
astar(Start, Goal, Closed) :-
        write(' What is the estimated cost from '),
        write(Start),
        write(' to '),
        write(Goal),
        nl,
        read(Fn),
        !,
        explore(Goal, [ [Start, [], 0, Fn] ], [], Closed),
        follow(Start, Goal, Closed).
```

```
/************************************************
 *                                              *
 *      Name:  follow                           *
 *                                              *
 *      Description: follow pointers back from Goal node to Start *
 *                   node returning the solution path            *
 *                                              *
 *      Inputs: [arg1] the Start node           *
 *             [arg2] the Goal node             *
 *             [arg3] the list of node on OPEN  *
 *                                              *
 *      Outputs: [arg4] the solution path from Start to Goal  *
 *                                              *
 ************************************************/
```

```
follow(Start, Start, [ [Start | _] ]) :-!,
        write('The path is from '),
        write(Start).
follow(Start, Node, [ [Node, Pred | _] | T]) :-
        follow(Start, Pred, T),
```

```
        !,
        write(' to '),
        write(Node).
follow(Start, Node, [H I T]) :-
        follow(Start, Node, T).
```

```
/*********************************************
*                                            *
*    Name: explore                           *
*                                            *
*    Description: Explores the nodes on OPEN, taking the first *
*                 node on OPEN and test to see if it is the Goal *
*                 node return CLOSED as the list of nodes that *
*                 have been visited. If OPEN is empty then the *
*                 Goal is inaccessible via Start node, otherwise *
*                 get the successors of first node on OPEN.   *
*                                            *
*    Inputs: [arg1]  the Goal node           *
*            [arg2] the list of nodes on OPEN *
*            [arg3] the list of nodes on CLOSED *
*                                            *
*    Outputs: [arg4] OPEN nodes after explore and expand *
*             [arg5] CLOSED nodes after explore and expand *
*                                            *
*********************************************/
```

```
explore(Goal, [], Closed, Closed) :-
        write(' All nodes visited '),
        write(Goal),
        write(' not found.'),
        nl.
explore(Goal, [ [Goal, Pred, Cost, Estim] I T], Visits,
                        [ [Goal, Pred,Cost] I Visits]) :- !.
```

explore(Goal, [[Node, Pred, Cost, Estim] | T], Closed, Visits) :-
    expand(Goal, [Node,Pred,Cost,Estim], T, Open, Closed),
    !,
    explore(Goal, Open, [[Node,Pred,Cost] | Closed], Visits).
explore(Goal, [[Node, Pred, Cost, _] | Open], Closed, Visits) :-
    explore(Goal, Open, [[Node,Pred,Cost] | Closed], Visits).


```
/************************************************
*                                              *
*      Name: expand                            *
*                                              *
*      Description: Expand  finds all the successors of a node, *
*                   pruning the list by removing those nodes *
*                   already on CLOSED, the unvisited nodes *
*                   are then processed and added to OPEN. *
*                                              *
*      Inputs: [arg1]  the Goal node           *
*              [arg2] node with accumulated cost from Start *
*              [arg3] the list of nodes on OPEN *
*              [arg5] the list of nodes on CLOSED *
*                                              *
*      Outputs: [arg4] the list of OPEN nodes after expansion *
*                                              *
************************************************/
```

expand(Goal, [Node, _, Cost, _], Open, New_open, Closed) :-
    findall(X, (path(X,Node, _); path(Node, X, _)), Descend),
    cleanup(Descend, Closed, Succs),
    write(' The unvisited successors of '),
    write(Node),
    write(' are: '),
    write(Succs),
    nl,
    process(Goal, Node, Cost, Succs, Open, New_open).

/* remove nodes already closed from successor list */

```
cleanup([], _, []).
cleanup([Quad I T], Closed, Cleaned) :-
     closed(Quad, Closed),
     cleanup(T, Closed, Cleaned).
cleanup([Quad I T], Closed, [Quad I Cleaned]) :-
     cleanup(T, Closed, Cleaned).
```

/* check if a node is on CLOSED */

```
closed(Node, [[Node I _] I _]).
closed(N, [_ I T]) :-
     closed(N, T).
```

```
/***********************************************
*                                             *
*     Name:  process                          *
*                                             *
*     Description: Finds estimated cost from each successor to  *
*                  goal and decides whether to put on OPEN.  *
*                                             *
*     Inputs: [arg1]  the Goal node           *
*             [arg2] the node whose successors are processed  *
*             [arg3] the cost of reaching the node from start node*
*             [arg4] the list of successors   *
*             [arg5] the list of OPEN nodes   *
*                                             *
*     Outputs: [arg6] OPEN nodes after processing successors  *
*                                             *
***********************************************/
```

```
process(_, _, _, [], O, O) :- !.
process(Goal, Node, Cost_to_n, [Succ | T], Open, New_open) :-
     (path(Node, Succ, Cost); path(Succ, Node, Cost)),
     estimate(Succ, Goal, Est_to_goal),
     !,
     Cost_to_succ is Cost_to_n + Cost,
     Total_estimate is Cost_to_succ + Est_to_goal,
     putinopen([Succ, Node, Cost_to_succ, Total_estimate],
                                        Open, Open2),
     process(Goal, Node, Cost_to_n, T, Open2, New_open).
process(Goal, Node, Cost_to_n, [Succ | T], Open, New_open) :-
     (path(Node, Succ, Cost); path(Succ, Node, Cost)),
     write(' What is the estimated cost from '),
     write(Succ),
     write(' to '),
     write(Goal),
     nl,
     read(Est_to_goal),
     Cost_to_succ is Cost_to_n + Cost,
     Total_estimate is Cost_to_succ + Est_to_goal,
     putinopen([Succ,Node,Cost_to_succ,Total_estimate],
                                        Open, Open2),
     process(Goal, Node, Cost_to_n, T, Open2, New_open).
```

/* decide whether to put the node on OPEN, or whether it is
necessary to change the pointer if the node has already been put
on OPEN, putting it in order */

```
putinopen([Node, Pred, Cost, Est], Open, New_open) :-
     opened([Node, Pred, Cost, Est], Open, New_open).
putinopen([Node, Pred, Cost, Est], Open, New_open) :-
     putinorder([Node, Pred, Cost, Est], Open, New_open).
```

```
/************************************************
*                                              *
*     Name:  opened                            *
*                                              *
*     Description: Test to see if a node is on OPEN, if it is and  *
*                  previous route is shorter than new route then   *
*                  leave OPEN unchanged; otherwise delete the *
*                  old quadruple and put the new quad on OPEN*
*                  in ascending order of total estimate to goal    *
*                                              *
*     Inputs:[arg1] the quadruple to put on OPEN               *
*            [arg2] the list of nodes on OPEN                  *
*                                              *
*     Outputs: [arg3] the new list of OPEN nodes              *
*                                              *
************************************************/


opened([Node, Pred, Cost, New_est],
               [[Node, Pred2, Cost2, Old_est] | T],
               [[Node, Pred2, Cost2, Old_est] | T]) :-
     Old_est =< New_est, !.
opened([Node, Pred, Cost, New_est],
               [ [Node, Pred2, Cost2, Old_est] | T], New_open):-
     !,
     putinorder([Node, Pred, Cost, New_est], T, New_open).
opened(Quad, [H | T], [H | New_open]) :-
     opened(Quad, T, New_open).


/************************************************
*     Name:  putinorder                        *
*                                              *
*     Description: Puts nodes on OPEN in ascending order of   *
*                  total estimate to goal, from start via the nodes *
*                                              *
```

```
*       Inputs:[arg1] the quadruple to put on OPEN           *
*               [arg2] the list of nodes on OPEN             *
*                                                            *
*       Outputs: [arg3] the new list of OPEN nodes           *
*                                                            *
*************************************************************/
```

```
putinorder([Node,Pred,Cost,Est], [], [Node,Pred,Cost,Est]]):-!.
putinorder([Node, Ptr, Gn, Est],
              [[Node2, Ptr2, Cost2, Est2] |T],
              [[Node, Ptr, Gn, Est],
               [Node2, Ptr2, Cost2, Est2] |T] ) :-
       Est < Est2.
putinorder(Quad, [H | T], [H | New_open]) :-
       putinorder(Quad, T, New_open).
```

Test the program by entering the following query

```
?- astar(paris, vienna, Visits).
```

CHAPTER 15

Natural Language Parsing

Natural language processing consists primarily of syntax analysis and semantic analysis, in this chapter we look at the first of these processes, syntax analysis, otherwise known as natural language parsing.

Consider translating from English to Russian and vice-versa, the following sentences:

The spirit is willing but the flesh is weak

We may get back:

The vodka is good but the steak is not so good.

Or the adage:

Out of sight, out of mind.

returning

Invisible idiot.

Can you imagine the problems with:

You are the apple of my eye.

Natural language processing (NLP) is a relatively new discipline, one of the goals of which is to enable the user to communicate with the computer in a language that they, the user, are familiar with, i.e. natural language. Textual input of natural language is what we will be looking at in this chapter. Once textual input of natural language has been achieved to a satisfactory level then we will be some way towards voice input. This is quite appealing because it means that there would be no complicated languages to learn. All we have to do is tell the machine what we want and it either does it or says it cannot do it. Communication with the computer via direct speech has its own problems in addition to those posed by textual natural language processing. It must be said that such commercial speech input systems will be here sooner or later but it is difficult to say exactly when.

Definition of terms

Syntax   'Grammar'

> *the part of grammar concerned with the arrangement of words in a sentence.*

Semantics 'the study of meaning'

> *The science of social and psychological effects of language. Classification of changes in word meanings*

Pragmatics 'the way we see the world'

> *Concerned with practical consequences as opposed to dogmatic (relating to an article of belief).*

Why bother with NL processing?

There is no need for a formal language because we are already experts in natural language. Natural language provides good and natural communication for some applications, e.g. database querying. Research into NLP must continue to remove present limitations. Technology is improving allowing sophisticated speech understanding with less restraints.

Research into NLP may provide useful insights into processes and representation of language in the human mind, thus heading towards true AI.

Problems with NL processing

The most difficult part of problem solving is defining a logical solution. Once defined, conversion to a formal language is relatively easy. It has not been possible to define a logical solution for all aspects of NLP.

Natural language is loose, vague and ambiguous, consequently natural language systems are large and unwieldy, with overheads on efficiency making a full system extremely slow.

Language is dynamic, in a constant state of flux, therefore unrestricted NLP is likely to remain a problem for some time. What is required is a subset of natural language that facilitates communication in all domains, but a useful subset is a long way off; commercial subsets tend to be domain dependent.

If our expert system, with the use of synthesized speech offered incorrect advice then there is the danger that the user may be tricked into believing the advice to be well founded by virtue of the intelligence it assumes the system has because it 'speaks'.

The major problem in NLP, however, is that we still do not fully understand the human natural language process.

Structural constraints in English

➡ Words cannot be arranged in an arbitrary order and still maintain the meaning inteded by the originator, or even make sense. There are fairly strict rules for ordering words in a sentence. These rules are called **grammar rules**.

For example, contrast the following sentences

Thrilling is a subject grammar.

Grammar is a thrilling subject.

➡ The acceptability of sentences does not depend solely upon meaning, e.g.

The wet happening, that bred a bulldozer, hued with a grown purple.

➡ There is even a correct way to use nonsense words; the following sentence almost sounds acceptable by virtue of the keywords in the 'right' places.

The gronk was plowny and the splugen carn flinked in the jabell.

Syntax

Syntax is a description of the way in which words must be ordered to make structurally acceptable sentences in a language. Every natural language has a syntax. There are many ways of describing syntax. By means of the ordering

➤ **word groups:**

nouns, adjectives, verbs, adverbs, etc.

➤ **word classes:**

nouns	happiness, table, Bob . . . . .
adjectives	red, happy, one . . . . .
verbs	kick, run, pray . . . . .
adverbs	quickly, once . . . . .
pronoun	it, he, they . . . . .
conjunction	and, but
preposition	to, on, from . . . . .

➤ **phrases:**   There are rules for describing phrase structure,
e.g. a noun phrase consists of

❏ an article
❏ any number of adjectives
❏ a noun
❏ and perhaps a prepositional phrase

A notation for describing phrase structure

NP   -> (ART) (ADJ*) Noun (PP)

ART   -> a I an I the

ADJ   -> large I green I redI angry I . . . . .

Noun -> house I idea I man I Carlton . . . . .

PP   -> Prep NP

Prep   -> off I in I against I on I . . . . .

Note, some classes of words are closed (e.g. art and conjunctions), others are open (e.g. adj and noun). The same notation can be used for collections of phrases, e.g. a sentence, which could be a concatenation of a noun phrase and verb phrase.

S -> NP VP

Parsing

A parser is a formalism which can determine whether a sentence (or string of words) conforms to the constraints of a language, and also builds a representation of the syntactic structure. This need not be a natural language. A programming language has rules for the ordering of tokens (reserved words, identifiers and symbols). The first pass of a compiler is often the parsing stage, checking that the syntax rules of the programming language have been adhered to.

A simple parser can be modelled after the transition network formalism:

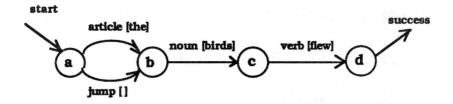

The above transition network will successfully parse sentences of the form:

S --> (art), noun, verb

    e.g.   birds fly

              the birds fly

              the man eats

but not: the black birds fly

What we need is the definition

    S --> (art), (adj*), noun, verb

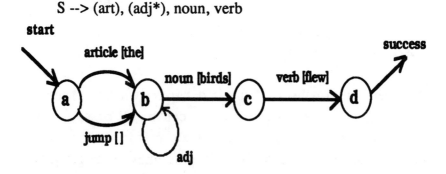

Parsing with Prolog

Consider the context free grammar. By context free we mean that the context in which the words are used is not known. The only knowledge available during the parse is knowledge about the word/phrase orderings.

    sentence --> noun_phrase, verb_phrase

    noun_phrase --> article, noun

    verb_phrase --> verb, noun_phrase
    verb_phrase --> verb

```
noun --> doctor
noun --> patient

article --> the

verb --> questions
verb --> doctors
```

The grammar is able to parse the following sentences:

The doctor questions the patient.
The patient questions the patient.
The doctor doctors the patient.

.

.

A naive Prolog parser can be written to parse these sentences. The chosen approach is to put the list of words to be parsed into a list and pass it to a predicate which tests for a sentence. Within each predicate **append** is used to generate pairs of lists which when concatenated produce the list of words to be parsed. For instance, when parsing a sentence **append** generates pairs of lists testing the generated lists to see if they constitute a noun phrase and a verb phrase, if they do then we have successfully parsed. If they are not a noun phrase followed by a verb phrase then generate another pair of lists, and repeat the test until the test succeeds or there are no more pairs of lists that can be generated.

```
sentence(S) :-                        /* S is a sentence if */
    append(NP, VP, S),  /* generate 2 lists NP & VP from S */
    noun_phrase(NP),          /* and NP is a noun phrase ? */
    verb_phrase(VP).          /* and VP isa verb phrase ? */
```

```
noun_phrase(NP) :-                      /* NP is a noun phrase if */
    append(Art, N, NP),          /* generate 2 lists Art and N */
    article(Art),                      /* and Art is an article */
    noun(N).                              /* and N is a noun */


verb_phrase(VP) :-                      /* VP is a verb phrase if */
    append(V, NP, VP),       /* generate 2 lists V and NP and */
    verb(V),                              /* V is a verb and */
    noun_phrase(NP).            /* NP is a noun phrase */
verb_phrase(V) :-
    verb(V).


noun([doctor]).
noun([patient]).


article([the]).


verb([questions]).
verb([doctors]).
```

We could make the query:

```
?- sentence([the, doctor, questions, the, patient]).
```

This is however very inefficient, because **append** will generate a pair of lists that we then go on to test. Most of the tests will fail, which means that we spend a lot of time backtracking to append, generating pairs of lists, and testing the generated lists.

A more efficient parser

Instead of splitting the string using append and then testing the fragments, we pass the whole string to a predicate, which consumes as many symbols as it needs to succeed, and returns as an argument the rest of the string. The rest of the string could be passed to another predicate.

For example:

> ?- noun_phrase([the,doctor, doctors, the, man], R).

succeeds with R = [doctors, the, man]

If we rewrite our parser so that all the predicates leave a list of the words remaining after the phrase has been removed then our parser is now:

```
sentence(S, Rest) :-  /* remove the sentence from S return Rest */
      noun_phrase(S, VP),  /* remove the noun phrase from S */
      verb_phrase(VP, Rest).  /* remove verb phrase from VP */

noun_phrase(NP, Rest) :- /* remove noun phrase from NP list */
      article(NP, Noun),   /* remove article from words in NP */
      noun(Noun, Rest). /* remove noun from words in Noun */

verb_phrase(VP, Rest) :-   /* remove verb phrase from VP list */
      verb(VP, NP),             /* remove verb and noun phrase */
      noun_phrase(NP, Rest). /* leave any extra words in Rest */
verb_phrase(V, Rest) :-    /* remove verb from words in list V */
      verb(V, Rest).

noun([doctor I Rest], Rest).
noun([patient I Rest], Rest).

article([the I Rest], Rest).

verb([questions I Rest], Rest).
verb([doctors  I Rest], Rest).
```

The query is now:

sentence([the, patient, questions, the doctor], []).

or

sentence([the,patient,questions,the,doctor,other,words],Excess).

Excess = [other, words]

Where the variable Excess is the list of words remaining after the sentence has been removed from the front of the list of words. In the example above the variable.

The Prolog grammar rule notation

Prolog provides a convenient and shorthand notation for the preceding parser. This is called the *Prolog grammar rule notation.*

sentence --> noun_phrase, verb_phrase.

noun_phrase --> article, noun.

verb_phrase --> verb, noun_phrase.
verb_phrase --> verb.

noun --> [doctor].
noun --> [patient].

article --> [the].

verb --> [questions].
verb --> [doctors].

Computing the parse tree

As parsing progresses, we might wish to build a representation of the structure of the sentence, instead of just being told 'yes'. This can be accomplished by using an extra argument in each rule to represent the structure parsed by each rule.

For example:

```
sentence([s, [NP, VP]]) -->
     noun_phrase(NP),
     verb_phrase(VP).


verb([v, [questions]])) --> [questions].
```

As Prolog clauses:

```
sentence([s, [NP, VP]], Sent, Rem) :-
     noun_phrase(NP, Sent, Rest),
     verb_phrase(VP, Rest, Rem).

verb([v, [questions]], [questions | Rem], Rem).


     sentence([s, [NP,VP]]) -->
         noun_phrase(NP),
         verb_phrase(VP).


     noun_phrase([np, [Art, N]]) -->
         article(Art),
         noun(N).


     verb_phrase([vp, [V, NP]]) -->
         verb(V),
         noun_phrase(NP).
```

```
verb_phrase([vp, [V]]) -->
    verb(V).

noun([noun, [doctor]]) --> [doctor].
noun([noun, [patient]]) --> [patient].

article([art, [the]]) --> [the].

verb([verb, [questions]]) --> [questions].
verb([verb, [doctors]]) --> [doctors].
```

The query is

?- sentence(Tree,[the,doctor,questions,the,patient],[]).
Tree will be instantiated to a representation of the structure:

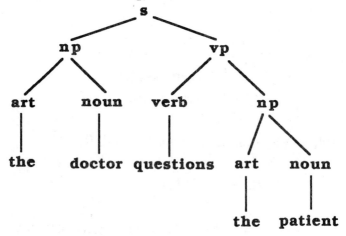

which is instantiated to:

```
[s,    [np,   [art, the],
              [noun, doctor] ],
       [vp,   [verb, questions],
              [np,   [art, the],
                     [noun, patient]
]      ]     ]
```

A predicate for printing out trees in a similar form is provided below. This predicate prints the tree on its side, to reflect the structure of the sentence.

```
print_tree(Tree) :-
       print_tree(Tree, 1).

print_tree(, _) :- !.
print_tree([H | T], Spacing) :-
       Indent is Spacing + 10,
       printrest(T, Indent),
       print_tree(H, Indent).
print_tree(Item, Spacing)
       put(13),
       tab(Spacing),
       write('-- '),
       write(Item).

printrest(, _) :- nl.
printrest([H | T], Spacing) :-
       printrest(T, Spacing),
       print_tree(H, Spacing).
```

The argument is the structure representing the sentence.

Extra arguments

Extra arguments can be added as illustrated in the last example, where the parse tree is computed. In each case the parse tree for each subtree (each predicate), was an argument to the grammar rules.

There is no limit to the number of arguments that can

occur in the goals using the grammar notation, there is however, the convention that all goals must have the same number of arguments.

In the previous example of returning the parse tree, it would not, for example, be possible to have a rule with zero arguments in any of the goals, or any number of arguments other than one.

If this convention is not adhered to, then the effect will be that the Prolog clauses that the grammar rule notation translates to, will be of differing arities. The parser will therefore not behave as expected.

Suppose we add the noun 'doctors' to our vocabulary

noun --> [doctor].
noun --> [doctors].
noun --> [patient].

We allow the following two sentences to be parsed

The doctor doctors the doctors.

and

*The doctors doctors the doctor.

*The doctors doctors the patient.

We need to add the verb 'doctor' to our vocabulary, i.e.

verb --> [doctor].

This will provide the correct parses:

The doctors doctor the doctor.

The doctors doctor the doctors.

but does not prevent the two ungrammatical sentences above, from being parsed successfully by our naive parser. It in fact introduces further ungrammatical sentences, namely:

*The doctor doctor the doctor.

* denotes ungrammatical sentences

What we need is some way of checking whether the subject is singular or plural, and checking whether the verb is consistent with the plurality of the sentence.

We can modify our parser in the following way:

```
sentence(P) -->
     noun_phrase(P),
     verb_phrase(P).

noun_phrase(P) -->
     article(P),
     noun(P).

verb_phrase(P) -->
     verb(P),
     noun_phrase(Q).
verb_phrase(P) -->
     verb(P).

noun(singular) --> [doctor].
noun(plural) --> [doctors].
noun(singular) --> [patient].
```

noun(plural) --> [patients].

article(_) --> [the].

verb(singular) --> [question].
verb(plural) --> [questions].
verb(singular) --> [doctor].
verb(plural) --> [doctors].

The syntax of the sentences would now be consistent but there are no pragmatic or semantic checks to forbid:

The patient doctors the doctor.

We could have both the parse tree and the singularity of the sentences checked, using the following version of our parser:

```
sentence([s, [NP,VP], P) -->
    noun_phrase(NP, P),
    verb_phrase(VP, P).

noun_phrase([np, [Art, N]], P) -->
    article(Art, P),
    noun(N, P).

verb_phrase([vp, [V, NP]], P) -->
    verb(V, P),
    noun_phrase(NP, R).
verb_phrase([vp, [V]], P) -->
    verb(V, P).

noun([noun, [doctor]], singular) --> [doctor].
noun([noun, [doctors]], plural) --> [doctors].
noun([noun, [patient]], singular) --> [patient].
```

noun([noun, [patients]], plural) --> [patients].

article([art, [the]], _) --> [the].

verb([verb,[questions]], singular) --> [questions].
verb([verb, [question]], plural) --> [question].
verb([verb, [doctors]], singular) --> [doctors].
verb([verb, [doctor]], plural) --> [doctor].

Finally suppose we had several verbs, it would become extremely tedious to have to put an entry in to the database for all of the possible forms of the verb depending upon the tense.

For example suppose we want to have:

doctor	question
doctors	questions
doctored	questioned
doctoring	questioning

Instead of adding the eight entries under verb, we store the stems and get Prolog to work out if the endings are valid or not, that is

```
verb_stem(doctor).
verb_stem(question).

verb --> [V],
         verb_stem(V) .
verb --> [V],
         (
             name(V, Tensed_verb),
             verb_ending(Stem, Tensed_verb),
             verb_stem(Stem)
         ) .
```

```
verb_ending(Stem, Verb) :-
      append(Stem, "s", Verb).
verb_ending(Stem, Verb) :-
      append(Stem, "ed", Verb).
verb_ending(Stem, Verb) :-
         append(Stem, "ing", Verb).

verb_stem(doctor).
verb_stem(question).
```

The correspondence of the verb endings could be checked through the use of an additional argument which conveys information about the tense of the verb.

It is worth noting that a single Prolog goal need only be enclosed within braces (curly brackets).

Multiple Prolog goals need to be enclosed within round brackets as well as braces because of the precedence and binding of the comma.

Glossary

ancestor

An ancestor of a goal is the goal's parent or its parent's parent etc. For example if we have the following database:

    a :- b.
    b :- c.
    c :- d.

then a, b, and c are ancestors of d.

anonymous variable

An anonymous variable is a variable that is written in a special way to show that it is different from every other variable in the clause. Another way of regarding the anonymous variable is as a variable whose value we are not interested in. It is written '_'. If we consider the following clause

    a(_, _).

there are two variables whose values we are not interested in (the two variables can be equal), whereas in:

    a(X, X).

There is only one variable.

argument

An argument of a goal or query is one of the terms written in brackets after it. The arguments of

   a(1, two, Three).

are 1, two and the variable Three.

arity

The arity of a goal or query is the number of arguments it has. The arity of a predicate is the number of arguments that the head of the clause has. The arity of:

   a(1, two, Three).

is 3.

atom

An atom is an object referred to by name. Anything that begins with a lower case letter and consists entirely of letters, numbers and the underscore character is an atom.

   two is an atom
   1 is not
   Three is not
   this_is
   _var is not an atom but a variable

backtrack

When Prolog answers no to a goal, it returns to the previous goal and tries to find another solution to it. This is called backtracking. If we have the following database:

    a(1).
    a(2).

    b(2).

and ask:

    ?- a(X), b(X).

then a(X) succeeds with X equal to 1, b(1) fails and so Prolog backtracks to find another solution for a, finding X = 2.

built in predicate

A built in predicate is a predicate about which Prolog can answer queries without any information being supplied by the user. The user cannot define clauses for a built in predicate, even if the predicate has a different arity.

clause

A clause is a piece of information Prolog uses to establish whether a goal is true. It will either say that a certain query is true, or that it is true under under certain conditions.

    a(1).
    a(X) :- b(X).

are both clauses.

consult

To consult a collection of clauses means to record them in Prolog's database so that they can be used for answering questions.

debug

To debug a program is to remove errors from it. The Prolog debugger is a tool that enables the user to watch each step of execution and thus to spot errors easily.

fact

A fact is a clause which is unconditionally true, that is once the clause has been matched the goal is proven.

a(1)

is a fact, but

a(X) :- b(X)

is not.

functor

A functor is the part of a goal or query that comes before the '('. Functors must obey exactly the same naming rules as atoms.

goal

A goal is something that Prolog is trying to prove (i.e. is searching for), either because the user typed it in, or because it needs it to prove something else. A goal can be an atom or a functor followed by some arguments separated by commas, enclosed in parentheses.

a(X, Y)

is an example of a goal.

last call optimisation

See tail recursion optimisation.

parent

When Prolog tries to establish a goal, it sometimes uses a rule that causes it to try other goals in the tail. The former goal is called the parent or the latter.

predicate

A predicate is collection of a clauses whose heads all have the same functor and arity. The predicate is referred to as:

functor/arity

for example:

length/2
findall/3

prompt

The prompt is the symbol, usually ?- used to indicate that Prolog
is waiting for the user to type in a query.

query

A query is the same as a goal but the term is more often used for
a goal entered by the user.

principal functor

In a complex structure like:

f1(f2(arg1,arg2, [arg3,f3(X),arg5,List]),

**   f4(1,2)).**

There are four functors, but when a search is made of the
database the search is made primarily for 'f1' - the principal
functor.

relation

A relation is a predicate with arity greater than 1. For instance:

christian(carlton).

christian is a property, but in

likes(masoud, books).

likes is a relation.

rule

A rule is a clause with one or more conditions. Thus:

a(X) :- b(X).

is a rule but

a(1).

is not.

side-effect

A side-effect is some effect caused by the proof of a goal other than the setting of variables. In

read(X).

X = term

the setting of X to term is not a side effect but the capturing of data from the input device (disc access etc.) is.

structure

A structure is something that can be decomposed into simple elements. Atoms, integers, reals and strings are simple elements whereas lists and trees, for example are structures.

tail

The tail of a rule is the part after the ':-'. Thus the tail of:

a :- b, c, d.

is b, c, d. b, c and d are called tail goals.

tail goal

See tail.

tail recursion

The recursive call in a predicate is the last subgoal of the tail goals.

tail recursion optimisation

A method of reducing the amount of space taken up on the frame stack. By conforming to tail recursion optimisation conditions space taken up by a parent goal can be overwritten by the tail goal. Hence recursive execution can be infinite. This facility does not exist on all implementations.

top-level interpreter

The top-level interpreter is the part of the system that accepts queries from the user and prints the answers.

variable

A variable is something that has not been assigned a value or whose value has been removed by backtracking. Variables are written using an upper case character or underscore character ('_') as the first character, and may be followed by letters and digits.

X is a variable

Var is a variable

_ is a special type of variable (see anonymous variable)

_123 is a variable

_var is a variable

1 is not a variable

3_Four is not a variable

aTOM is not a variable

Solutions

Chapter 3

1. greet:-
       nl,nl,
       write(' Who am I greeting ? '),
       nl,nl,
       read(Who),
       nl,nl,
        write(' Hello '),
       write(Who),
        write(' !'),
       nl,nl.

2. get0(X),put(X),nl.

Chapter 4 Solutions to BIP Questions

1. pop(S,I) :-
         Struct =.. [S,I],
         retract(Struct).

   push(S,I) :-
         Struct =.. [S,I],
         asserta(Struct).

2. stacker(Arg):-
         Arg =.. [push,Stack,Item],
         Struct =.. [Stack,Item],
         asserta(Struct).
    stacker(Arg):-

```
        Arg =.. [pop,Stack,Item],
        Struct =.. [Stack,Item],
        retract(Struct).
    stacker(Arg):-
        Arg =.. [Op,Item],
        Struct =.. [Op,pile,Item],
        call(Struct).
```

3. eman(P):-
```
        name(P,L),
        reverse(L,R),
        name(X,P),
        write(X),nl.
```

Chapter 5

1. count([],0).
```
   count([_|T],X) :-
        count(T,Y),
        X is Y + 1.
```

2. triangle(1,1).
```
   triangle(N,S):-
        M is N - 1,
        triangle(M,R),
        S is M + R.
```

Chapter 6 Solutions to list exercises

Head	Tail
a	[b, c]
H	[T]
a	[]

[a, b,c]	[]
[1, 2]	[[3, 4]]
5	[[6, 7, 8]]
[bat, cat, rat]	[[red,yellow,green], [the,quick,brown,fox]]

Chapter 7

1.   parent(X, Y):- mother(X, Y).
        parent(X, Y):- father(X, Y).

        ancester(X, Y):- parent(X, Y).
        ancester(X, Y):-
                parent(X, Z),
                ancester(Z, Y).

2.   last([X], X).
      last([_ | T]) :- last(T).

3.   reverse([], []).
      reverse([H | T], Z):-
              reverse(T, L),
              append(L, [H], Z).

4.   member(X, [X | _]).
      member(X, [_ | T]) :- member(X, T).

5.   shuffle([],L,L).
      shuffle([H | A],B,[H | C]) :- shuffle(B,A,C).

Chapter 8

factorial(Number, Factorial) :-
      fact(Number, 1, Factorial).

```
fact(0, Sofar, Sofar).
fact(Num, Sofar, Factorial) :-
    M is Num - 1,
    Intermediate_result is Sofar * Num,
    fact(M, Intermediate_result, Factorial).
```

Bibliography

Alvey, P. 1982
A programme for Advanced Information Technology, The Report of the Alvey Committee, HMSO.

Clark, K. L. & McCabe, F. G. 1982
"POPLOG : A Language for Implementing Expert Systems" Machine Intelligence 10, Ellis Horwood.

Clocksin, W. & Mellish, C. 1982
"Programming in Prolog" Springer Verlag.

Duda, R. O. & Gaschning, J. G. 1981
"Knowledge-Based Expert Systems Come of Age" in Byte, September, 1981.

Kay, A. 1984
Work and Play : A discussion,
The AI Business, Winston and Prendergast (Eds.) MIT Press.

Shortcliffe, E. H. R. 1976
Computer-based Medical Consultations : MYCIN. American Elsevier.

Sloman, A. Hardy, S. & Gibson, J. 1983
"POPLOG : A Multilanguage Program Development Environment"
Information Technology : Research and Development, Vol. 2.

Winston, P. & Horn, B. 1980
"LISP" Addison Wesley.

Index